TEACH SOUL-WINNING

TEACHER'S GUIDE FOR SOUL-WINNING MADE EASY

by

C. S. Lovett

M.A., M. Div., D.D.
president of Personal Christianity

Author of

Soul-Winning Made Easy
Dealing with the Devil
Witnessing Made Easy
"Help Lord — The Devil Wants Me Fat!"
Latest Word on the Last Days
Longing to Be Loved

Published by

PERSONAL CHRISTIANITY
Box 549
Baldwin Park, California 91706

ISBN 0-938148-12-5
1984 EDITION

© C. S. LOVETT 1962

No part of this book may be used or reproduced in any manner whatsoever without written permission of the copyright owner except in the case of brief quotations in articles and reviews.

To
"The Spirit of Christ"

Who has imparted to us the "Encounter Method" of soul-winning and without whose ministry all that is presented here is worthless.

Printed in the United States of America

Contents

Preface
"One Who Dared" ... 4

Chapter One
"Let's Get the Facts Straight" ... 6

Chapter Two
"Demonstrated Power!" ... 23

Chapter Three
"The Power of the Plan" ... 39

Chapter Four
"Back to the Lab" ... 55

Chapter Five
"FEAR—It's Got to Go!" ... 63

Chapter Six
"Get 'em Going" ... 72

"Just for You" ... 77

Questions Most Frequently Asked in Soul-Winning Classes ... 78

ONE WHO DARED!

Here is Rev. H. Edward Rowe, associate pastor of the more than 4000 members of the great Church of the Open Door in downtown Los Angeles. Obedient to the Holy Spirit, this remarkable pastor asked that his people be taught the "Encounter-Method" of soul-winning. Not since the days of R. A. Torry and the church's founder, had anyone been invited to teach a soul-winning skill to the congregation. I was pleased to accept the invitation.

This is startling when you think of it. How often does the pastor of a nationally known church invite an outsider to come and teach a vital skill to his people? The Holy Spirit has to direct such a thing. This outstanding man of God made this rare move. And now that great church is alive with people skilled in the "Encounter-Method" of presenting Christ alive!

This book reflects the spirit of the great seminar held there. Some of the pictures are actual scenes taken in the classes. As you read, see if you can't sense the excitement that filled the place. Enthusiasm runs high when the people of an evangelistic church find themselves equipped with the actual techniques for doing the job the Lord Jesus gave to us all.

There is nothing to match the thrill of winning a soul to Jesus. But that thrill can be multiplied when you teach others how to do it. Imagine the power that came to this great church as the members began to take hold of this skill. As this is being written, an army of trained workers stands ready to harvest the unsaved who are attracted to this famous evangelistic center. Here is pastor Rowe's own estimate of the work you are about to consider...

"The unique method of Brother Lovett was the most effective thrust in getting our people to witness for Christ that has ever been offered in my tenure of ministry at the Church of the Open Door. We are seeing the results."

H. Edward Rowe

C. O. D.—SCENE OF THE GIANT SEMINAR.

STUDENTS READY FOR THE SKILL.

Chapter One

"LET'S GET THE FACTS STRAIGHT"

IN THE FIRST SESSION YOU:

- Present a panorama of the course.
- Outline the basic truths of soul-winning.
- Create an appetite for training in the students.

The first hour offers drama-lecture type orientation. The students mean business, coming, perhaps, as a result of the motivation filmstrip or publicized word of your ability to equip them with this skill.

GREETING

A good number have arrived and the clock orders you to begin. If you are not the pastor, and should he be in charge, advise him you will need the full time. Let him introduce you right after someone has led in prayer. This allows hearts to become quiet and expectant.

Introduce yourself.

"Good evening. We are here to discuss the biggest business of all — men meeting their God. But first I would like to meet you."

- In your hands you hold the registration cards gathered after the showing of the filmstrip. Prepare to call them off. As each name is read, have the person stand for the others to see. If different groups or organizations have people present, have someone identify them.

> **NOTE:** If the class contains more than 25 students, recognize only various groups present. Note also, having the students stand allows you to cull the registration cards. Absentee cards should be set aside and a written invitation mailed out during the week. It is not too late for people to enter the second session.

- Be professional in your attitude. Regardless how much or how little you know about soul-winning, your people need to feel the man before them has something to offer. They need to feel confidence in you, so you must reflect self-assurance. You are there because you possess a skill, or at least the knowledge of that skill. And they will receive it before the seminar is ended. Read the discussion under "Your Attitude," on page 31 of "Visitation Training Made Easy." It tells why you must appear in full command.

"While I will be your teacher for the next five sessions, let me tell you of another teacher . . . "

TELL A STORY

An ancient philosopher, who was used to receiving large sums of money from those he taught, was approached by a poor lad who asked to become one of his disciples.

"What will you give in return for this?" asked the wise man.

"I will give you myself," was the reply.

"Very well, I accept the gift," said the philosopher, "And someday I will release you back to yourself a much more valuable person than you are now."

Apply it:

"Class, there is a sense in which you are putting yourself in my hands. If you will trust me to pass on to you what God has given me, you will depart richer and more valuable to the Lord. Now let's take a look at the course."

PANORAMA

- Pass out a copy of the red workshop folder to each person.

With this in hand and open to the inside, the student is ready to learn the scope of the course and what he can expect to receive. Explain:

"These folders give a panorama of the course and on the left hand side you will see the objectives listed. Do you all have them? Hold them up. Wave them. Ah, what a sight. (A cute ice-breaker.) **All right, put them down. Here's what we will be learning:"**

- Recite them aloud for the class.

"And now take a moment to look across the page and you will see why this class is valuable to you and to the Lord."

NOTE: This arrangement or order assumes the filmstrip has been used to enlist the students and you have the registration cards at hand. However, if the strip **was** not used, alter the procedure. Give the class a few moments to register. They do this by writing their names on the slips at the bottom of the workshop folders, tearing them out and passing them to the front. When this is done, you can gather them and call off the names for identification.

HINT: Some may prefer to wait and see if they like the course before turning in a slip. This is OK. Ask for them again at the end of the session and by that time they will have been "sold." Let them know it is all right to do this.

"Now let's set the folders aside and get down to business with a business question . . .

WHAT DOES IT TAKE TO BE A MILLIONAIRE? Anyone can answer. (Wait for response. Some will say money — wealth — and finally, out will come, 'A million dollars.')

What did you say? (Reply, "A million dollars.") **Right. And now Class, if one must have a million dollars to be a millionaire, what must one have in order to be a Christian? Tell me in one word."** (Pause while the answer comes.)

"Christ."

"Good. The word to note is H-A-V-E. What does that spell?"

A SIMPLE SIGN — AN IMPLANTED TRUTH!

8

> **NOTE:** It sounds simple to have the class respond in this fashion, but reciting the "HAVE" aloud, gets them in the act. Then as they reply, reach into your supply box and bring forth a placard or poster with the H-A-V-E in the center of it. Hold it up and then place it in the chalk rail of an easel standing near you. Thus, the word has been presented to the ears, has been on their lips, and now the eyes will pick it up to send to the brain as an image.

"This brings us to the basic truth of soul-winning — that Salvation is in a Person!"

> **NOTE:** On another piece of board about 2½ feet long, write the phrase SALVATION IS IN A PERSON and place it in the chalk rail over the other one and leave it there while the subject is being discussed.

SALVATION IS IN A PERSON

Discussion

● Here is the grand truth of the "encounter-method." Do not hestitate to depart from tradition in presenting this method. A new frontier has been opened and you are free to make the truths clear any way you can. There are no pioneers to copy. You are the pioneer.

● Many mistakenly feel salvation has to do with accepting the Bible or truths **about** Christ. The doctrine of His Virgin Birth or divinity, for example, are thought to contain salvation and clinging to these somehow brings eternal life. But none of these can save anyone, for the Saviour is a **Person** — not a doctrine.

The world offers countless religions with each claiming to be the true one. How is a person to identify the correct one? An examination reveals all of them want men to **believe something** whereas the Bible asks men to **receive Someone**. There is a big difference between believing something and receiving someone. One is merely an opinion, while the other, an experience.

But Satan is clever. He has fooled people into thinking they are saved if they believe in something, it doesn't matter what. "Only believe," is his counsel, and he doesn't care what it is as long as they do not commit themselves to the Living Christ.

They can believe the Bible and he is happy. They can believe many wondrous things **about** Christ, and he has no fear. They can trust in some sort of religious experience, and he is just as pleased. He is undisturbed until they start to do business with Jesus, personally. Therefore the course begins with the grand truth that Jesus is alive and waiting to come into men's hearts **at this moment.**

● The Lord Jesus, Himself, found this truth difficult to impart. Recall His journey to Bethany after Lazarus had been dead for four days? And remember that Martha the sister of Lazarus met Him on the outskirts of the village and cried, "Lord, if thou hadst been here, my brother had not died?" Then Jesus sought to comfort her, "Thy brother will live again." But she answered, "I know that he shall rise in the resurrection . . ."

Then Jesus brought a remarkable lesson. It was as though He said to her, "Martha, get your eyes off the **doctrine** of the resurrection and get them on Me," and now we quote," for I AM THE RESURRECTION AND THE LIFE" . . . (John 11:25). Martha was face to face with the Resurrection and didn't know it. She was looking into the "eyes" of Eternal Life and missed the point.

A familiar verse, yes, but how many have noticed that the Resurrection is a **Person?** Who has realized that Eternal Life is in a Person? Poor Martha failed to see the point of the doctrine she knew so well. Thus it is that even the Bible, with all its doctrines, can save no one.

This at once explains why Christianity is so satisfying. Men can have an actual experience with the One who said, "I am the way, the truth and the Life" (John 14:6). Meeting the Living Jesus is the feature that throws the religions of the world into the junk pile. For regardless of the claims of Mohammed, his body is yet in the tomb and one can go and see where he is buried. The same is true of Buddha and Confucius as well, but there is an empty tomb in Palestine, because Christ Arose! This same Jesus knocks on the door of men's hearts and says, "If you will open the door, I will come in!" Here is the most exciting and glamorous business in the world . . . presenting Jesus at the door of a human heart.

● This is your point. If life is in the Person of Christ, then one must HAVE Christ in order to be saved. Observe for the class the forceful way the Apostle John declared this: "He that hath the Son hath life and he that hath not the Son of God, hath not life" (1st John 5:12 A.S.V.). There are two kinds of people in this world (and the next), the haves and the have nots.

"All right class, If Salvation is in a Person, then Soul-winning is introducing that Person. This is logical, isn't it? Men must meet Christ before they can have Him."

SOUL-WINNING IS INTRODUCING THAT PERSON

Discussion

NOTE: Replace the old sign now, with the new one.

● With it clearly established, Salvation is in a Person, it follows logically that soul-winning is introducing men to Jesus. The soul-winner is an **introducer.** Thus, your students will be learning the skill of introducing men to Christ. This is the second basic truth of the "Encounter-Method."

● Demonstrate this truth by asking two men in the front row their names. Then turn immediately and introduce them to each other. Another overly simple stunt? Of course, but it crystallizes the idea.

"Soul-winning is just like that, only then we are saying in effect, 'I'd like to have you meet the Lord Jesus Christ.'"

STORY

Brother Lovett tells this story.

When I was 21 years old the phone rang one day. I answered and the voice said, "Cummings?" I said, "Yes." The voice replied, "This is your father speaking." What a shock that was! I had never seen my dad. We made an appointment and minutes later I met him for the first time in my life!

Apply:

"Now class, it is a tremendous thing for a man to meet his father for the first time when he is 21 years old. But it cannot compare with the experience of meeting the One Who made you! That's big! And that is what occurs in the soul-winning introduction."

● This is the time to mention it would indeed be difficult to introduce someone to a person whom you did not know. Surprisingly enough, soul-winning classes often turn out to be the place where some, thinking they were already saved, actually meet Christ for the first time. Here, the matter is stripped of non-essentials and the encounter spotlighted. People can see at once where they stand when the mechanics of salvation are laid bare.

"But there is something peculiar about the soul-winning introduction. In fact, when you think about it, it appears a stupid business. Notice. Here we are telling people that Jesus, whom they cannot see with their eyes, is waiting to come, of all places, into their hearts. Now doesn't that sound a little ridiculous on the surface? Of course, and it would be stupid were it not for the ministry of whom?" (They answer this right away.)

"The Holy Spirit!"

"Right. Soul-winning would be laughable were it not for the work of the Holy Spirit. It is His job to make Christ real. No amount of eloquence on the part of a worker can make Christ real. No dramatic skill, plan or psychology can do that, for it is the exclusive ministry of the Holy Spirit. Therefore, nothing you will hear from me or gain in this class can ever be understood as a substitute for the work of the Holy Spirit."

● The next point in order is the fact that the Holy Spirit makes Christ real. But since a spirit-being is not visible to the human eye, He must be apprehended by some other means. This brings us to the work of the Holy Spirit. As there is no hand to grasp or voice to hear, a worker will find himself talking **about** Christ unless he knows the Holy Spirit is simultaneously speaking to the prospect's heart in the moment of introduction.

"How would you introduce a spirit? Hold a seance? No, I am sure you will agree that no human can produce or introduce a spirit being. And the making real of Christ is a work that only the Holy Spirit can do."

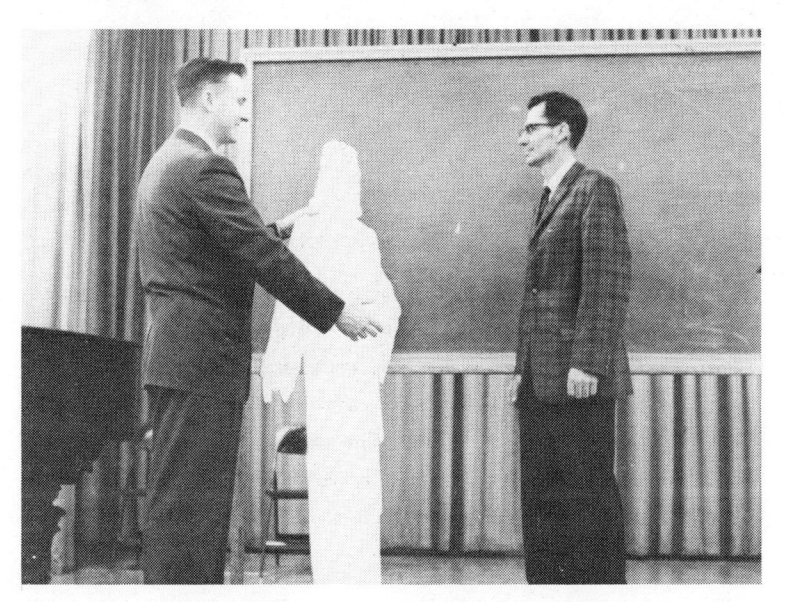

THE FIGURE DRAMATIZES THE SPIRIT'S WORK!

● In the days of His flesh, our Lord Jesus walked upon the earth bodily, and men could see and hear Him, but they could not H-A-V-E Him. It was not until He had finished the Atonement could He come to men as the "life-giving Spirit" (1 Cor. 15:45). Thus today, as the **Omnipresent** Spirit, He is able to come into any heart that will admit Him.

For His earthly ministry, He was introduced **to the world** by John the Baptist. But now, for His Spirit-ministry, He is introduced **to individuals,** by us. Since He is unseen, His presence must be certified by the Spirit of God. Therefore there can be no effective soul-winning unless one works with the Holy Spirit.

"But how does the Holy Spirit do this? In the very moment you speak to a person of Jesus, the Holy Spirit is also speaking. When you tell him Jesus is waiting to come into his heart, the Holy Spirit also says, "Yes, it is so." This is what makes it exciting. It is fascinating to watch men's eyes as you speak, for they give an indication of the Spirit's working. When you get used to working with Him, you will be able to interpret most of what people say and do in order to recognize the Holy Spirit's witness. It truly is amazing."

● Here is the fascination of soul-winning. A few years ago there appeared in "Life Magazine" the story of a Mid-western Tornado and a full page picture showed a piece of straw driven through a huge telephone pole. The photo was so amazing, that some in your class may remember it.

>   **HINT:** It would be easy to make a mock-up of this if you are handy. Use a soda straw and let a cardboard mailing tube represent the pole. Drill a hole to pass the straw through the tube and set the display before the class. Then ask . . .

"How could anything as weak as a piece of straw be forced through anything as rugged as a telephone pole?" (Let them work on the answer.)

The students will come up with the explanation. Here is a wonderful way to compare our weakness with the Spirit's mighty power. The answer, of course, is that the straw, while weak in itself, was totally surrendered to the wind. Thus, the power of the Tornado became the power of the straw through surrender. And so with the Soul-winner. Surrendered to God for soul-winning, he can move in the power of the Holy Spirit and do astonishing things. This is the adventure awaiting them.

With all boldness one can say, "Jesus is waiting to save you," and the prospect knows it is true. Regardless what he might say to the contrary, he knows Jesus is there. This is why the plan is called the "Encounter-Method." Whether the prospect likes it or not, he does meet Jesus. It is an encounter. Of course, what he **does with Christ** is his own business. He will answer to God for that. It is the faithfulness of the Holy Spirit that makes soul-winning possible and exciting. Oh, the fun of seeing doors open before your eyes — and watching hearts melt under His power — and then to feel Jesus' presence in that moment — it is wonderful . . . ' BUT

YOU NEED A PLAN
Discussion

● Bring forth a new sign to replace the "Soul-Winning is an introduction," that has occupied the easel. Now they are ready for the third point of your orientation lecture. If they can fully understand their helplessness **without** a plan, they will remain with you for all the sessions.

"This is the hardest work in all the world. There is a special agony for Christians in soul-winning. All of us have been near people and felt deep concern for them, but we were tortured with inward questions: 'How will I start the conversation? How will I bring up the subject of Christ and Salvation? What will I say? Oh, if only I could talk about the Lord.' And so it goes. Before long, both the time and opportunity have slipped away and you said nothing. But the agony is still there, 'Why didn't I speak out for my Jesus?' "

There is a fearful terror associated with soul-winning, when Christians do not **know how** to do the work. Because of this terror, 95% of all Christians have never led a soul to Christ. It is not because they do not care to speak, but mostly because they do not know how. People fear the unknown.

> HINT: Remind them of what they saw in the film-strip. Those who do not know how to swim are afraid of the water. Those who do not know how to handle firearms are afraid of guns, etc.

"People are always teasing Brother Lovett over the title of our textbook. They ask him, 'You say soul-winning is easy, maybe for you, but what makes it so hard for me?' and he always answers,

'Trying to do the work of the Holy Spirit.' Without a plan for soul-winning, people invaribly try to do the work of the Spirit and that is impossible. In this course, we will see that our plan for winning is actually a plan for working with the Holy Spirit. And when we truly learn to do this . . . it is easy. When you think about it, we need a plan for most everything we do."

> HINT: Again recall the film-strip. There we found one does not build a house without plans, the walls might not meet. One does not go into business without planning for so much capital, he might not get the door open. And even God has a plan for bringing men to Himself. How presumptious for men to think that while God needs a plan for His work — we don't.

- The advantages of a plan are wondrous. Have someone from the group open the soul-winning textbook to page 24 and read the list of 12 advantages. This gives you a break from speaking and allows someone else to be in focus for a moment.

Illustration.

When I was with the Air Force as an instructor, I would take each new class of cadets down to the flight line and introduce them to their twin-engine training plane. For the first few days, they did not take off, but remained in the cabin to become familiar with the instruments and controls. They memorized the location and use of everything in the plane. Then when it came time to fly for the first time, they were free from the worry of all those instruments in front of them and could concentrate on the sheer joy of maneuvering the plane through the sky.

Apply.

This points up one of the most wonderful advantages of a plan. When you know thoroughly what you are going to do and say to a prospect, you are free from having to concentrate on yourself and the struggle for words. You can concentrate on watching the Holy Spirit work. It is safe to say, most soul-winners have never seen Him operate. They have been too busy planning their next move to enjoy the Lord's presence or observe the prospect that closely.

"**A dedicated Christian, armed with his plan, is the finest tool the Holy Spirit has for bringing men to Christ. And a plan grants** men just that — the fun of working with the Holy Spirit. As you can cut more wood with a sharp axe than a dull one, so can the Spirit of God do more with a sharp soul-winner than with a dull one. In this class you will acquire such a plan — so get ready for the thrill of your life!"

LECTURE SUMMARY

Here again are the three facts you want to implant:
1. Salvation is IN Christ and men must H-A-V-E Him in order to be saved.
2. Men must meet Christ before they can have Him, therefore soul-winning is an **introduction.** Since no one can introduce a Spirit, it remains the exclusive work of the Holy Spirit to make Christ **real.**
3. To work with the Holy Spirit one must **have a plan.**

Since the "Encounter-Method" depends fully upon the Holy Spirit's ministry, these truths must become the property of your students. Taught here, in the first session, they become the springboard for all that follows. Now to cement them in their understanding.

"**All right, we have just discussed the basic truths of the Encounter Method. Now, without the help of the signs, see if you can recall what they are. Aloud, if you will, what is the first one? Anyone? Salvation is** . . . (Coach a bit and the response will come.)

TOOLS

1. Textbook.

"**Here is the principal tool of the course.** (Hold up a copy of the soul-winning book.) **This is the textbook and it is called "Soul-winning Made Easy." We have copies for everyone and I want each of you to secure a copy for himself, and in just a bit I will be giving you your first reading assignment."**

> NOTE: Unless a bookstore is serving the church and ready to supply the class, you will need to order the textbooks from the publisher in advance of the class. Order enough, so that there are plenty on hand for everyone. When the session is over, students will come up to the front of the class to your display table and make their purchases. There will be other items beside the text and these too should be a part of your preparation.

"Everything you need for personal know-how is in this book. Having it will free you from the necessity of taking notes and will insure the deposit of skill will remain with you long after this seminar is over. Also, it will cover things I will not touch upon in the class."

> NOTE: Some churches prefer to provide the books. This is good, but students should make some financial investment in the course. A tuition or offering can be used. People generally despise even valuable things, when they are free.

2. Testament.

"The next tool is a pocket-size New Testament. Maybe you already have a small Testament you could use, but type size is important. It should be large enough for a person to read when it is held in front of him. I use an inexpensive one like this (hold up your sample) so in case I am tempted to give it to a new Christian, I can do so without worrying about the cost."

- Make yourself a large mock Bible. It can be of cardboard and glued to give the appearance of a Bible. Hinge the cover so you can turn it back. Construct pages with lettering on them to resemble printing. On each of the four pages, letter out a verse. (See photo.) Place the tabs so they work from the top down.

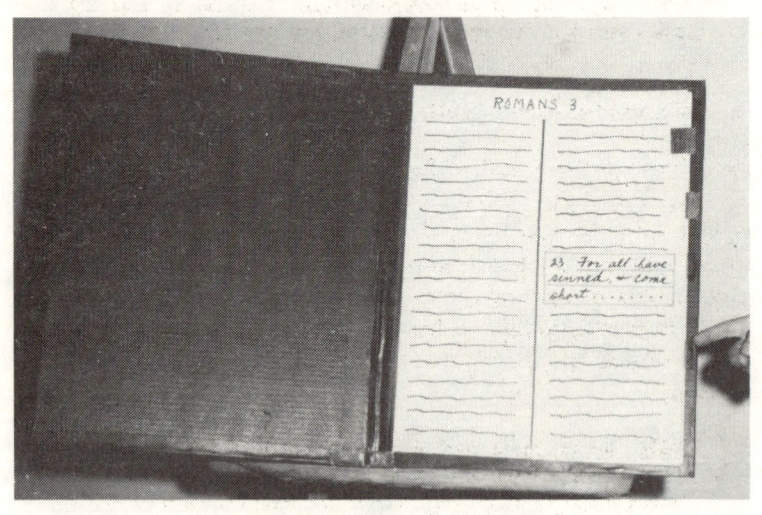

THE TABS MAKE THE DIFFERENCE.

"The plan you will be learning uses four verses. And once you begin to use them in your soul-winning interview, there will be no time for hunting through the pages for the right one. If you do this . . . (Make a hasty, finger-licking search and fan the pages as though desperately searching for a verse. The class will roar, but they get the idea) . . . **Satan will get in a question and you are off target. Therefore you will need the tabs so you can switch from verse to verse with a single motion of the hand, like this"** . . . (Demonstrate the maneuver.)

> NOTE: Inasmuch as there are 4 verses, there will be 4 tabs. Place them so the right thumb can hold down the tab while the book is flipped open to the left. They are all placed so the Testament opens the same way each time. The verses are boxed with red ink and show up to the reader instantly.

"Once you start through your plan, you move like a well-oiled watch, tick . . . tick . . . tick . . . and you move from verse to verse with clocklike precision. Take a good look at my big dummy here and then tab your own Testaments at home and bring them with you next time."

> HINT: Suggest they use a library mending tape or a "Magic" mending tape. Do not use cellophane tape. The adhesive runs and pages soon stick together. Any recording splicing tape is good also.

3. Items to leave with the new convert.

● Hold up the 3 tools: "Beginning To Live", "Lovett's Lights On 1st John" and "Salvation Clear and Plain." Explain they are to be left with the new Christian. Often the soul-winning interview is so dramatic and emotional-laden, what is said is overshadowed by the awesomeness of meeting Jesus. Your counsel is lost unless you put these compact helps into his hands. These allow him to go back over the experience of meeting Jesus and handle any doubts that come to mind.

> NOTE: Do not spend much time presenting these 3 items, but encourage them to come up and examine them for themselves as well as reading the comments in their textbook. You are eager to get on to the challenge of the first session.

ACTION.

"Now we are going to have a 3rd grade exercise. You will be tempted to laugh, but this is a precious way to fix things in our minds. I am going to state for you a transition phrase. I will do it one line at a time, and after I say it, we will say it together. All right. here's the first . . . (Break up the phrasing so that it is easy for them to follow along.)

"If I were a good friend of yours and came over to your house — knocked at the door and wanted to come in — what would you say? All right then — the Lord Jesus is waiting to come into your heart right now — will you open the door? — will you let Him in?"

>NOTE: These are the hardest words to say, but the most powerful the Holy Spirit can use. As your students read their texts, they will see why.

"Now that you have caught the swing of this, I am going to let you bring the precious challenge of the soul-winning ministry to yourselves. Usually, teachers challenge their students, but this time you will challenge yourselves. Here are the four lines of a poem. I will recite one line at a time and then we will repeat it together:

>'When I enter that beautiful city —
>   And the Saints in glory draw near —
>I want someone to greet me and tell me —
>   It was you who invited me here.'"

"Isn't that a blessed thought? Would you like to learn it? All right, let's do it again. (Go through it a couple of times with them. They will want to learn it.) **This course is to be your guarantee of that experience.**"

"And now here is your assignment . . . "

ASSIGNMENT.

1. Secure a copy of the text (hold it up) and read to page 85 for next time. You will need to do this to gain the most from our next class.

THE TEXT — A TOOL FOR LIVES!

NOTE: Do not hesitate to ask your people to buy the text. This is the best insurance your work will abide. Our Lord Jesus conducted His famous seminar upon the Mount and it would be lost to us today, were it not for His Textbook, the Bible. We can go to it and refresh ourselves as we hear His voice repeating the things He said there. And you can do the same. As the Lord protected His investment with a book, so will your work ring in their ears everytime they pick up "Soul-winning Made Easy."

2. Provide yourselves with the Pocket-size Testament and tab it. Then underscore the verses in red. They are listed in your text. Do it as I showed you in the big mock Testament.

Cutie:

"If you are thinking, 'Boy, this is a lot of trouble just to learn how to win souls,' there is a way out. I have an excuse slip for you (a laughter release will follow this). **I know it sounds humorous, but this is serious, for the excuse is signed by Satan himself** (you are smiling, of course). **The ushers will give one to each of**

you. Read it — and if you can say, 'God helping me, I am going to learn how to introduce people to Jesus,' then it will not apply to you. But save it and pass it on to someone who does need an excuse."

"As soon as we are dismissed, you can come and secure your supplies. And now brother . . . , will you ask God's blessing upon us as we are dismissed."

DISMISS.

> HINT: After you finish speaking, slip a breath sweetener into your mouth. Speaking for 30 minutes or more changes the breath chemistry and you could offend without knowing it. Have them in your pocket so you will be ready for those who come up to you immediately after dismissal.

THINGS TO BRING.

> Supply of workshop folders for registration
> Flashcards or placards for truths
> Large Mock Testament with tabs
> Copy of the Soul-Winning book to hold up
> Your personal Testament to display
> Fear certificates
> Roll of mints for yourself
> Camera to snap the action for publicity
> Three items to leave with new convert

ARRANGE BEFOREHAND.

> The pastor's part in the opening service
> Table for your books and displays before the class
> Ushers to hand out panoramas and fear certificates
> A lapel or throat mike if the crowd is big
> Someone to take pictures for the bulletin board
> An easel to hold your flash cards
> Man to lead in prayer
> Get there early to set things up
> A watch or clock to keep on schedule.

Chapter Two
DEMONSTRATED POWER!
IN THIS LESSON THE STUDENTS:
- Learn the controlling factors of any soul-winning plan
- Observe the distance traveled during a soul-winning interview
- Get the feel of the approaches and the plan

GREETING
You watch the class gather, but the clock says it is time to begin. You know punctuality pays. Even though people are still moving about and perhaps in the doorway, you ask someone to lead in prayer. It seems strange to you to do this, but you mean business for Christ and every minute is precious. The crowd settles at once.

"May I see the hands of those who are here for the first time. Fine. Will the ushers see that they get registration slips, please? Be sure and detach the slips, fill them in and get them to me at the end of the class."

STORY
A young lad and his dad were camping in the woods not too far from a village and decided to stay out an extra week. The father asked the boy to carry a letter back to the village in order to let his office know of the change in plans. "But Dad," questioned the youngster, "I don't think I know the way?"

"Do you see the trail leading to the big tree atop the next ridge there?"

"I see the way that far."

"Well, when you get there, you will see the trail dropping down into a big meadow. Then, when you get there, the trail goes directly into the village."

Apply:
"Perhaps you're wondering how I am going to make soul-winners out of you with a few foundation truths and a tabbed New Testament. Well, we have come as far as the big tree and

in this session we will drop down into the meadow and from there you will see the trail that will allow you to "go to town" on your own."

"Do you all have your soul-winning books? Hold them up, let's see them."

> NOTE: This makes a nice shot for the bulletin board. Your man with the polaroid camera is busy. You have already alerted him. In fact, you furnished him with a list of the scenes you wanted. These could enlist others in the class.

REVIEW QUESTIONS

"Now let's see what we gained from the last time. I'll ask a few questions and anyone can respond. If the answer pops into your head, just sound off. Okay, here's the first.

1. "What did we say Salvation was? Anyone? (Ans. Having Christ.)

> HINT: Make yourself five large size letter "A's". Cut them from cardboard say, 5 to 7 inches high. As soon as the first person gives a correct answer acknowledge with, "Right," and toss him one of the "A's." It is amusing and new sparkle is added to the review session.

2. "What word did we emphasize last time?" (Ans. H-A-V-E)
3. "What is soul-winning? That is, what did we call it?" (Ans. An introduction)
4. "What is the work of the Holy Spirit that makes this introduction possible?" (Ans. He makes Christ real to the prospect.)
5. "What did we say we needed in order to work with the Holy Spirit?" (Ans. A plan)

> HINT: Secure a wind-up toy auto. Wind it before the people as you say, "Here is what a worker looks like without a plan." And then let the wheels go. They spin madly in the air. "He may be full of Scripture verses, but without a plan he gets nowhere. But give him a plan and he . . . (now wind the auto again and let it race across the floor) . . . gets there fast!"

● With the questioning under way, the ice melts. People find it fun to respond and appreciate your warm reaction to their

24

answers. Even if someone should give an unrelated response, avoid a negative reply. Instead, nod your head to one side and say, **"Well, that's an idea,"** or **"That's a thought,"** or **"Who else has a comment?"** In your class, **no one is ever wrong.** Find a positive way to handle each response and soon your people will explode with answers. **A squelched student often fails to respond again.**

● Emphasize they will be learning but one plan in this seminar.

This is not a course on soul-winning methods, but one method or plan for working with the Holy Spirit. We live in an age of specialization where it pays to know one thing and know it well. When you are finished, your students will not be experts, but they will be specialists. They will know how to introduce someone to Christ. Later, when they have gained the skill from you, they will be adapting it to their own personalities and perhaps changing it a bit to fit their own ego strengths. But the plan, as it is, becomes their starting point.

NEW MATERIAL

● **Factors controlling soul-winning plans.**

The questions are finished. Now they are to meet some serious truths which can alter completely their concept of soul-winning. Move slowly and gently and watch the reactions in their faces. You could be trespassing long-held views and the Holy Spirit will use your gentleness and unassuming attitude to ease them onto higher ground. Your discussion begins with the Person of the Lord Jesus. Every truly born again person is mellowed with the thought of Him.

THE PERSON OF JESUS

"What you think of Jesus governs the way you introduce Him."

> HINT: With those words, move over to your standing figure of the Lord. In a cuddly manner, bring "Him" closer to yourself and begin a description of the sweet graces found in the splendid Person of our Lord.

JESUS IS MORE THAN A DOCTRINE NOW!

"If you have found Him to be the most gentle Person you have ever met — who is so kind He melts your heart with His goodness and generosity — so patient He waits years for you to finally give Him your life — so sweet and understanding, you wonder how anyone could be afraid of Him — so unselfish He gives you His own Name and Glory — so longsuffering He will take abuse from you and return it with favor instead of anger. If you have found Him as One who has not only loved you enough to die for you, but has dedicated His life to you; and Who is so much in love with men, HE receives them tenderly regardless of what they may have ever said or done to Him — if you behold Him this way, then there are three approaches you would NOT USE in introducing Him to others."

"In presenting these negative approaches to you, I do not mean to belittle those who use them. Also, I am exaggerating them and mentioning extremes for the sake of clear teaching. I know you will understand. The first we call the . . . "

- **POUNDED ALTAR METHOD.** This method is the situation at the altar where someone has responded to the Gospel and a worker kneels alongside. In his zeal, but without knowledge, he begins to shout in the ear and pound the respondent on the back reciting such phrases as, "Pray through brother," or, "Have you got it yet?" or, "Feel anything yet?" or, "Keep on praying, you'll get it."

  Of course, that is no way to introduce anyone, let alone someone as gentle and warm as Jesus. These people mean well, but have no real knowledge as to what to do. In this ignorance of Jesus' tenderness and splendor, they carry on a meaningless exercise. They hope it will accomplish something, but they are not just sure what. In the meantime, the respondent isn't sure either. Once you learn the eagerness of Jesus to receive men, this type of work is eliminated immediately. It is replaced with a Spirit-controlled introduction.

- **FUMBLE METHOD. "The next is the fumble method and you will understand why when you see it demonstrated. Mr. ....will you come and stand here, please?"**

ACTION:

For this demonstration use a prepared script. It is perfectly all right to have it in hand as you give the demo. Or, it can be memorized ahead of time for smoothness. The two of you stand before the class and you open the conversation . . .

"It has been wonderful to spend time with you to talk about Christian things, but I wish you would accept Christ . . . even now." Prospect: "Maybe I should, but this seems to be an important matter. I'd better think it over. I don't make important decisions without first sleeping on them. You know the old slogan, 'Before you invest, investigate?' Well, that's me."

"Oh . . . ah . . . (Then pull a worker's catalogue from your pocket and take a couple of seconds to find the appropriate answer) . . . **It says here, 'Now is the accepted time, now is the day of Salvation!'**" (You stumble and hesitate as if embarrassed a bit at not knowing what to say.)
Prospect: "Well, what about tomorrow? Won't it keep a day?"

"Well . . . uh . . . (Now hastily look thru the index of the worker's guide once more and then let it slip from your hands to the floor. As you retrieve it, apologize for the delay and continue:) . . . **it says, "Boast not thyself of tomorrow for thou knowest not what a day may bring forth."**
Prospect: "What do you want me to do?"

"Ah . . . er . . . (Find the place where it says, 'Repent and be baptized.')

Prospect: "How do I repent? And how can I be baptized now?"

"Well . . . uh . . . I . . . (Then disgusted, shove the guide into your pocket) **I know if you will just pray and ask God to forgive you, He will.**" (Demo is ended.)

"Thank you Mr. .... for helping me. I know you found that amusing class, but I mean it only to show that we do not need a catalogue of verses to introduce someone to Jesus. Does anyone remember what Mr. Lovett said in the book about his experience with verses? It was on page 21."

● Soul-winning and Scripture memorization are separate fields.
If one is going to debate and argue, he needs verses as ammunition. But, in soul-winning, the work is done by the Holy Spirit. The objective is to **confront** men with Christ, not **convince** them. This ministry concentrates on the skill of introducing Christ and the Holy Spirit takes it from there. A catalogue of verses cannot help.

● **SLEDGE HAMMER METHOD.** From its hiding place, produce a rubber hammer and reach over and tap (lightly, of course,) your helper on the head. The class will roar.

"**You can almost guess the name of this next approach which we do not use. It's the 'Sledge Hammer Method.' I am sure you have heard of it. It is where you grab a man like this . . .** "

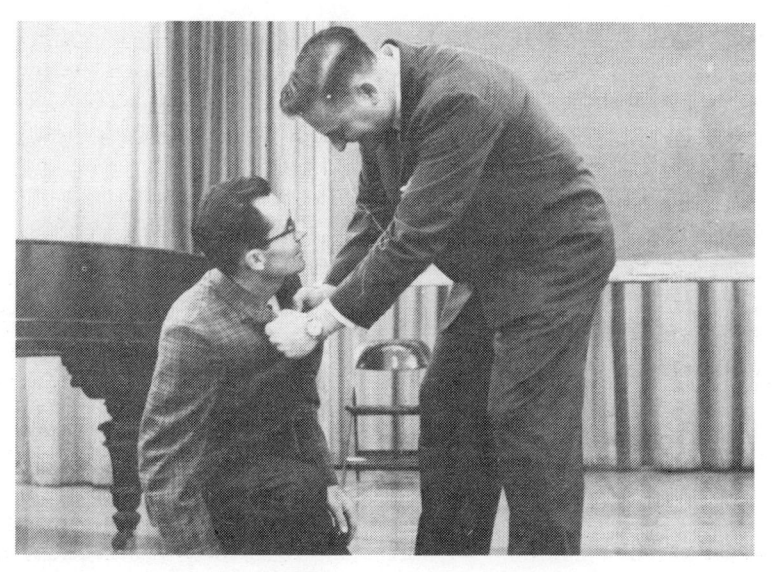

THIS DEMO BRINGS A VOLUME OF TEACHING.

ACTION:

Seize Mr._____by the lapels of his coat as you ask, "Are you born again? Do you know that unless you repent you are headed for hell! You need Christ to save you and if you do not call on His Name you are headed for a terrible doom. And, except you repent you will die in your sins and spend all eternity in torment and misery and anguish. Do it now for the wrath of God abides on you . . . " and so on. As you speak these words to your helper, he has been coached to sink lower and lower until you have him on the floor. The class will laugh, but the point is received.

"Class, when you consider the gentle and precious nature of our Lord Jesus, it must govern our view of soul-winning. You have laughed at these methods which I have demonstrated, but they are used all the time. I cannot help but feel that the users lose sight of our Precious Saviour and forget the kind of a Person He is."

THE NATURE OF MAN

"This last demonstration has taught us something else, however. Not only must we consider the Person of Christ, but also the nature of man. Now it is true, you can walk up to a man and tell him he will perish AND THE HOLY SPIRIT WILL BACK YOU UP. He will certify your statements at once, but that is not the problem. The man cannot take it. You see, it is not enough to know the Holy Spirit bears witness, we must also know something of the nature of man."

STORY

(Maybe you have a suitable one.)

One day Brother Lovett was driving along a fast boulevard and as a truck passed him, the driver tossed out a coke bottle. It struck the windshield squarely before our brother's face. Instinctively he ducked. He didn't expect it, it surprised him. Therefore, he was startled and ducked. It was a good thing he did, for he was showered with splinters of glass. But this is why we duck, isn't it? We are startled or afraid of getting hurt.

Apply:

"Perhaps all of us have passed a car while going through a puddle and the spray hit our windshield. What did we do instinctively? We ducked. Maybe it was a newspaper that flew up off the road or a branch from a tree, but the reaction is the same. Unless we're prepared, — **WE DUCK!** (Make a ducking motion with your hands flung up to protect your face.) **And so it is with soul-winning; if we suddenly come upon people and present Christ without warning or preparation — what will they do? . . . Duck!"**

- **Man is a tripartite being.** (1) He is intellectual, that is, he has a mind and is a thinking creature. (2) He is emotional. He has feelings that move him and prompt his actions. (3) He is capable of decision. Thus, he is a volitional creature as well.

30

These three aspects of human personality are important when we speak of soul-winning. It is not enough to know about the Lord, one must know about man too.

> **HINT:** Make 3 flashcards. One each for **INTELLECTUAL; EMOTIONAL; and VOLITIONAL.** Display each in your chalk rail as you discuss the separate features of human personality.

● Confront a man with a panic situation and his decisions will likely be emotional rather than intellectual. They will be dictated by his feelings rather than his reason. Whenever too much emotion is present, without reason, the resulting decisions are always emotional. On the other hand, if one comes to conclusions about Christ, by way of reason alone, his decisions will be purely intellectual and no more valid than emotional ones. Genuine decisions require both elements. A man must not only be stirred and motivated but also know clearly what he is doing, or the resulting decision will not involve his entire being.

TRUTH ON DISPLAY.

To burst upon a man and confront him with an astonishing demand of God, violates the law of human personality. The man is not ready to handle such staggering news that instant, but he will be, if you make a gradual approach that allows his **mind** to travel the distance comfortably. This does not mean a long time is required. Indeed not, it can take just minutes. Therefore in soul-winning, where a staggering idea is presented, we must meet a man **where he is** and take him **intellectually where we want him to go.** When he arrives at the decision point, emotion and reason will combine to produce a good decision.

● In soul-winning, emotion is supplied by the Holy Spirit. When the prospect suddenly becomes aware that the One who made him is standing just outside his heart's door, that's big! In fact, almost overwhelming as the Holy Spirit bears witness. But the man is ready to handle it, if he has been intellectually prepared.

We watch our Lord do this as He deals with the woman at the well in John, Chapter Four. His conversation with her began with a cup of water and He brought her systematically to the place where she could consider her Messiah before her face! Notice the awful impact of His last words to her: "I that speak unto thee am He!" Had the conversation begun with that staggering announcement, the poor woman would have fled in terror. She would have ducked!

"We say that crudeness and failure to understand the kind of a Person Jesus is can lead to awful technique. But now we find, the nature of man, if it is ignored, can lead to overwhelming clumsiness. It is just as important to understand the nature of man as it is to appreciate the Person of the Lord Jesus."

GOING THE DISTANCE

● As soon as your students appropriate the fact human personality is tripartite, with both reason and emotion needed for valid decision, you are ready to present the soul-winning encounter **visually.** Use a large blackboard. Do not fuss with your drawing to make it pretty. In fact, the more crude the better. Otherwise the students may be attracted to your artwork and miss a point. Quickly draw a line across the board. At the left end, inscribe 3 short, vertical lines. (See photo.) Say to the class:

"**In soul-winning we must meet a man where he is** (tap the board at the point of the three vertical lines) **and take him systematically through the steps** (now make 4 more short, vertical lines at spaced intervals across the board) **and bring him to the place where he can consider Christ at the door of his heart.** (Put an X at the extreme right end of the line) . . . **here. What I want you to notice is, that this is some distance!"** (Chalk an arc from one end of the line to the other.)

> HINT: Gesture with your hands as you face the class. "We are meeting people here . . . (move your left hand to the extreme left) . . . and taking them all the way over to here . . . (Move your right hand to the extreme right) . . . and that is a long way."

"When you think about it, this is precisely what salesmen do. They approach you with talk of the weather, your house, some news, your car, etc., then they take you systematically through a number of conversation points finally bringing you to the place where you are obligated to consider their product. Is this not so? Do they not secure your interest and then maneuver you to a decision concerning their merchandise? Of course. Believe me, they have plans and they memorize them cold. They have to — they travel so far in bringing you to decision."

● It is some distance from the beginning of a soul-winning interview to the point where Christ is presented. And since one cannot immediately thrust himself upon another, he needs a calculated approach to ease the prospect into a Christ-centered conversation. And since the distance to be traveled is great, neither can he spend much time at any one point. He must get through the steps, fast, FAST, F-A-S-T, as the Anacin people say. Thus, the soul-winner must be skilled. Some sophistication is obviously needed, but that is why you are there.

● In the next lesson the work of the Holy Spirit will be emphasized. In fact, over-emphasized, if that is possible. What you seek now, is for the students to learn that a prospect is actually **maneuvered** from non-interest to the point where he can encounter Christ. And that requires skill. People are not easily maneuvered, except by those who know how. It amounts to a manipulation of another person, but it is done in the power of God. That will be the focus of your teaching next time. It is enough for them to see the distance they travel must be covered systematically.

> HINT: If the students apprehend this material, you have gained much ground. These features alone are enough to shatter traditional views of soul-winning and your students will undergo serious mental experiences as they begin to register. You are breaking up hard ground. One cannot honestly learn when hindered by preconceived judgments.

THE APPROACH

"Now we are ready to learn the plan. And you will find when this plan is skilfully used, men must meet Christ. It is not a plan for CONVINCING people about Christ. No, the Holy Spirit does that. It is a different concept — the objective is to CONFRONT men with the Living Saviour. When it is done properly, men find themselves face to face with Christ, as the Spirit bears witness to His presence, and they must DO SOMETHING with Him. That is the secret of all we will gain in this seminar."

"Now as we go through the material, do not try to learn anything this session. Just relax and see if you can't sense the 'feel' of it. Say to yourself, 'I'll just watch this time and see what the Holy Spirit indicates to me.' Don't take any notes for all that you will see is here (hold it up) in your textbook. Of course, those of you who have read the assignment are ready for the plan."

● Two men can meet and without any outward effort, a soul-winning interview is under way. What appears to be a casual incident, is actually the calculated result of using an approach. The "Encounter-Method" has three approach questions that work like a shoehorn. They slide a prospect into a Christ-centered conversation without his realizing it.

"The plan has 3 approach questions. They are psychologically worked out so that it does not matter how people respond. (Step to the blackboard and indicate the three vertical, short lines at the beginning of the long line.) **Here they are. They sound innocent and begin with a nonthreatening question. The threat increases with each one. Here's the first . . . "**

Three approach questions:
1. "Are you interested in spiritual things?"
2. "Have you ever thought of becoming a Christian?"
3. "What if someone were to ask you, 'What is a Christian?' What would you say?"

● Present these to the class exactly as they appear on page 44 of the text. The feature to stress is, regardless of the answer coming back from the prospect, the next question is in order. Your students will have questions now, i.e., what if a person says this or that? Show how they can go right on regardless of the query.

>   **HINT:** Have the class open their textbooks to page 51. Yours is open to the place too. Recite with them right down the list of things listed there. Note for them how the prospect has been measured spiritually and you have been positive all the way. Never once has he been told he was not a Christian.

"A staggering truth has just dawned upon your man and the answer that comes from him now will be an open door. His words will be an invitation to move right on with the plan."

ACTION:

You are ready to demonstrate. You have arranged for someone to act as the prospect. Have him come and stand beside you now. He will have very little to say so his role is easy. You will do most of the talking. A tension-releasing chuckle will float across the audience when you add, **"Is it OK if I lead Mr. ....to the Lord?"** They already know he is a dedicated man. It could be their pastor.

NOW THEY SEE THE PLAN!

> NOTE: Coach your man to give only bare yes and no responses.
> For the most part you will be saying, "The prospect will usually say . . . ,"then go on and give the answers you want from the prospect. This makes your demo go smoothly and keeps any distraction from being introduced.

"If it is OK with you, I'd like to read you 4 verses of Scripture and explain them to you and then you will know what a Christian is. That would be OK, wouldn't it?"

> HINT: Nod your head up and down as you say, "That would be OK, wouldn't it?" Then turn and looking at the audience, repeat the phrase and nod your head vigorously. You will begin to see heads bobbing all over the place. Then add the reason, "Man, you see, is a suggestible being. He responds to suggestion. In fact, I see heads nodding right now." The people will laugh, but now they see why you nod your head when you ask the question. It evokes the desired reply.

"Now, up to this point there has been nothing outward to indicate a soul-winning conversation was under way. No Testament is in sight and the questions have been asked in a casual manner. I know I sound a bit teachy when I demonstrate, but in

36

a live situation, it appears as normal conversation. Your man is not alarmed. Nothing is out of the ordinary. Your request to present four verses is acceptable . . . and then you draw your "six-gun" with the words:

"God says in His Word that we are all sinners, for we read . . . "

> NOTE: Now show the class how you pull your Testament from your pocket as you say those words. Flip to Romans 3:23 with a single motion of the hand. Do it several times so the audience can see how smoothly it is done.

* * * *

> The remainder of the demonstration is not included here. It is assumed the teacher has memorized the plan and can demonstrate it easily. If you doubt your ability, secure the cassette of the dialogue and memorize it. Word for word is the best way to present the plan for it will match the text. After your people have gained the skill, they can shape the plan to fit their individual personalities.

* * * *

"What you have just witnessed is powerful know-how. It is the technique of manipulating a person from the first contact to the place where he can consider Jesus at the door of his heart. But all you have seen is worthless apart from the Holy Spirit. Everything depends on His making Christ real. But now let's get your teeth to take a bite . . . "

LAB WORK

"Will you turn in your texts to page 110 and prepare to recite the 12 transition lines aloud with me? (Pause while they find the place) **All right, are you ready?** (Nod your head up and down and their response will bring another humorous, tension-release.) **Let's begin . . .** "If it is OK with you, I'd like to read . . . etc."

NOTE: You are holding a copy of the text before you and reading in phrases they can follow. People like the "feel" of hearing their voices in unison. It is a grand sound and prepares them for the time when they will be working with a partner in the first, out-loud practice sessions.

"Now you have seen the plan demonstrated. You have sampled the transition lines. Maybe some have thought it looks easy, but it isn't. There is a big gap between seeing it and doing it yourself. Your first try in the lab will convince you of that. Smoothness is very important, so here is your first assignment."

ASSIGNMENT

"Read to page 115 in the soul-winning book."

"At home, you will go through these 12 transition lines aloud several times. And then repeat the 4 verses aloud too. Memorize them, and as you do, use your Testament. Each time you recite a verse, flip the Testament to the place so that it becomes natural for you to synchronize your hands to your words. That's the way to get smooth."

"Be sure to bring your tabbed Testament with you next time. Then as I go through another demonstration for you, you can flip through the verses with me. Also, read through the soul-winning plan aloud. See if you can hear my voice as you do it."

Prayer - Dismiss.

WHAT TO BRING

1. Flashcards
2. Extra soul-winning books
3. Extra Workshop folders for newcomers
4. Large cut-out of Christ
5. Some kind of worker's catalogue of verses
6. Rubber (tire changing) hammer
7. Camera—pictures for bulletin board
8. Toy auto.

Chapter Three
THE POWER OF THE PLAN

THIS TIME YOU
- Emphasize the Holy Spirit's Work
- Observe the five cautions of soul-winning
- Begin lab-work with the plan

GREETING
The class gathers. You are ready to begin. This time you may elect to lead in prayer since you desire the Holy Spirit to reveal Himself in an unusual working. The people are settled.

"Good evening. You were so responsive last time, I know you are eager to see what the Lord has for you tonight. First, did you bring your Testaments? Are they all tabbed and ready to go? Let's see them. Hold them up. Fine."

> NOTE: A fine ice-breaker. They have done something together. And you also have another picture for the church bulletin board. A Picture such as this can be made to say almost anything depending on the caption you place under it, i.e., "The Soul-winning class with its fishing tackle in order."

STORY
Before the days of radar, ship captains developed sensitive ears to detect an echo from their ship's whistle and thus determine their position in a fog. The story is told of a captain caught in a dense fog on one of the Great Lakes. Suddenly his face became tense and he rang for the engines to slow down. His whistle shrieked once more and then he rang for the engines to stop. "There's something out there dead ahead," he exclaimed, "I get an echo." A landbound passenger standing nearby said, "I don't hear a thing." A moment later the fog lifted a bit. Not a dozen yards off the bow was a huge steel garbage barge that had broken loose from its mooring in the harbor and drifted out onto the lake. The captain's trained ear paid off!

Apply:
In the same way, soul-winners listen for the Holy Spirit! While the captain listened for the echo of his whistle, the soul-winner develops a similar sensitivity to the Spirit's working. The

more I am in this business, the more convinced I am the Holy Spirit does the work and our skill consists of working with Him. He uses us to make the introduction of Christ, but in His power. Our ears learn to hear things in the prospect's words that tell us the Holy Spirit is bearing witness. Our eyes learn to detect clues in his behaviour pattern which indicates He is speaking and we come to recognize quickly an opportunity created by Him. While the non-soul-winner may not notice a thing, there comes a moment when the fog lifts and a soul, newly born of the Holy Spirit, stands revealed.

"Now you may think that I am going over board on the Holy Spirit in this seminar. In fact, you may suspect I am a little nuts. But if I am, it is over the Holy Spirit and the Word of God. And most soul-winners are. When you think about it, what else do we have today? So don't be too surprised with yourselves if you get a little peculiar and become excited over the Holy Spirit's work in Soul-winning. There is nothing more thrilling."

REVIEW QUESTIONS

"Now let me take a sampling of your minds. I'll ask some review questions and you be prepared to snap back the answer. These might be a little harder than the ones asked last time, for we have moved deeper into the truths of the "Encounter-Method." Things are getting more "chewy" now. No one makes mistakes in this class. The first question is easy."

> NOTE: As soon as the first person responds correctly, pause a moment and say, "Correct, you were fast with your answer. Here's your "A" — Catch it." Make a tossing gesture with your hand as though throwing an actual "A" to the respondent, but now it is an imaginary one. "Did you get it? — By faith?" There's a pause and then a nodding head. Even this can be a teaching. "That's the way we receive Christ. We take Him by faith . . . in the same way." From now on you will not present any more cut-out "A's", but toss imaginary ones to reward your students. They love it.

1. "How many verses in this plan?" (Ans. Four.)

> RECALL: Here is the place to stress a strategic point. "Why do we use so few verses? Is it because we do not believe in the Word of God or Scripture memorization?" (Ans. NO! It is because they are all we need for an intro.) Recall for them that it is what a person DOES with Christ that finally counts. Therefore they are not learning to preach, debate or argue — but simply to introduce Jesus. And since the Holy Spirit does the real work, our part can be minimized.

2. **"Last time we demonstrated 3 approaches NOT TO USE. What did we call the one where . . .**

    a. A man is slapped on the back and one shouts in his ear, "Pray through brother?" (Ans. The Pounded Altar approach.)

    b. A catalogue of verses is used to reply to objections? (Ans. The Fumble approach.)

    c. A man is button-holed with a sudden, overwhelming challenge for Christ? (Ans. Sledge-hammer approach.)

3. **"To whom (or what) did we liken the soul-winner?"** (Ans. Salesman.)

    > RECALL: A salesman comes to your home and begins with a point of contact. He comments on your house, nice lawn, children etc., then he begins a canned pitch. He controls the conversation and brings you to the place where you are asked to decide for his product. He manipulates you. He maneuvers you. He handles you. The soul-winner does the same . . . he manipulates people in the power of God. It is a skill.

4. **"We said any soul-winning approach must consider two things. What was one of them?** (Ans. The PERSON of Jesus — The NATURE of man.)

    > RECALL: If you behold Jesus as a sweet, gentle Person who is eager to be loved of men and humble enough to throw His arms about the worst of them, this governs the way you will introduce Him. But man's nature is a governing factor too. We found him to be an INTELLECTUAL being . . . an (they'll respond) EMOTIONAL being and a . . . VOLITIONAL being. Unless a man knows what he is doing he cannot make a good decision. If it is all feeling, aroused under threat or panic, it will be an emotional decision which will wear away when the threat is gone.

NEW MATERIAL

Step to the blackboard and again draw the long line across the board. You are about to make another visual presentation of soul-winning.

"The steps of soul-winning generally follow this pattern. There must be an approach. In our case, we have 3 approach questions. (Make the 3 short, vertical lines again at the left end of the line.) Some form of the Word of God presented (Make another vertical line some space away. See photo); the conviction of sin (another mark on the board); the penalty for sin (another mark); Christ as the remedy for sin (mark); Christ is available (mark); Here He is (mark); Will you accept Him? (mark). And we have already noted that is some distance to travel!"

> NOTE: You covered the great distance traveled in soul-winning, but return to it again now. Students cannot appreciate the real truth of the Spirit's ministry unless this distance is kept in view. In their minds they are asking "How can anyone truly cover that much distance as fast as our teacher does it and feel a man can be really saved?" They will see in just a moment.

THE EYE-GATE TRAVELS THE DISTANCE!

"Now we travel this distance according to plan. If we don't, we won't get there. It's too far to go for us to be anything but systematic about getting there. The plan you are learning covers the same steps as any other soul-winning plan and . . . notice the real objective. Here! (Tap the board at the point of the last step.) Here is where we want to go. This is the critical point . . . 'will you let Him in?' This is the whole point of our working . . . this is the grand climax. Everything that is done is calculated to get us here. (Tap the board again.) **And if we are not systematic about it, we just won't get there. And this same thing applies whether we are selling merchandise or presenting our Lord Jesus."**

"The speed at which we can travel through the steps is the speed with which the prospect can lay hold of each step on the way. I know you are thinking of the verses that could prove each point and there are lots of them, but they are proved another way. Did you know the Holy Spirit travels that distance too? He goes with us along the same route and it is His work at each step that makes it possible for us to bring men to Christ fast—FAST—F-A-S-T! Therefore we can say this: While our work is described as systematic the work of the Holy Spirit is AUTOMATIC."

> HINT: Put these two words on separate flash boards. Use them before your people as you pronounce the grand truth that while our work is SYSTEMATIC, His work is AUTOMATIC. This is an urgent feature of the "Encounter Method" and must be a part of their working knowledge.

THE AUTOMATIC WORK OF THE HOLY SPIRIT

Discussion

● At the approach, the Spirit automatically grants the worker favor in the eyes of his prospect. One does not have to build a case for himself or sell the prospect on the idea of listening. In the moment you begin the approach, the Holy Spirit bears witness to your intentions. God announces you as His representative and respect for you, without any selling on your part, will be obvious.

- When the Testament is produced, the Spirit automatically bears witness it is the Word of God, so it does not have to be defended or explained in any way. For the matter of sin, it is unnecessary to pile Scripture verses in order to bring conviction. For in the moment a single verse is read, the Spirit automatically brings conviction. The prospect knows he is a sinner in spite of any words he offers to the contrary.

- When it comes to the penalty or wages of sin, the worker need not threaten. The very second it is pronounced, "The wages of sin is death," the Holy Spirit says, "Yes, that is true," and the unbeliever senses an awful fate awaits him. Of course, if he doesn't care, that is his own business. Yet, the unsaved man rarely argues the point, for he is under the convincing witness of doom.

- When a worker declares the gift of life in Christ, the Spirit says, "Indeed," and it is unnecessary to bring sermons on Christ or the cross. As for the presentation of Jesus at the door of a human heart, there is no way for us to certify this. For no one, but the Holy Spirit can make Jesus real. There is no way for a human to make any spirit real — He must reveal Himself.

- Finally, closing the deal. Here is why a salesman calls. He does not come to tell you how nice his product is and then, "So long, I'll see you sometime." That would be ridiculous. He says, "Will you buy?" One cannot tell of the wonder of the Christian life, the uniqueness of God's forgiveness with Christ waiting to come in and then, "Goodbye." No! That is the point of the whole business. "Jesus is waiting to come into your heart right now — will you let Him in?" Not only are these the hardest words to say, but they are the most powerful the Spirit can use. When those words are uttered, the Spirit grips the prospect's heart in a vise. This challenge also bears the certainty of God and a man knows he must **do something** with the Christ standing there — one way or the other.

"All right, let's go over them again. We have said there are at least seven things the Holy Spirit does when you begin to introduce anyone to Christ!

1. He bears witness your intentions are OK so you do not have to prove yourself.
2. He certifies the Word of God so you need not defend it.
3. He brings smashing conviction so there is no need to pile up verses.
4. He certifies the wages of sin is death, so no need for threats.
5. He verifies the need of Christ as Saviour, no need to dwell on it or teach the cross.
6. He makes Christ real; no need to sermonize about Jesus.
7. As you bring the appeal to admit Christ, He grips the heart in a vise. In those fateful seconds, silence can be as powerful as words.

EXERCISE

You have been lecturing steadily on the Holy Spirit and there is more to come. A break is provided if you pause and offer, **"I was pondering something today and maybe you can help me. I was trying to think of any place in the Bible where we are commanded to win souls. Can you think of any?"** This registers with a shock. You can almost feel some defensiveness arise. And the answers are not long in coming. They start out . . .

"He that winneth souls is wise."
"Yes, we are declared wise IF WE DO win souls."
"Go ye into all the world and preach the Gospel."
"Yes, Preach. We are told to preach all right."
"As the Father hath sent me, even so send I you."
"We're SENT, that's true. And more? Can you think of any place we are told to win?"
"The harvest is ripe."
"Yes, indeed. There are plenty of people out there."
"Go, make disciples."
"Yes, DISCIPLES."
"Ye shall be witnesses unto me."

"Yes, WITNESSES. But witnessing and winning are two separate sciences as you know."

"Well . . . none, huh? Any more?"

"Follow me and I will make you fishers of men."

"FISH, yes. We are to go fishing. (Pause) **You know it is beginning to look as if the Word of God teaches the Holy Spirit wins souls and we are simply instructed to go and present Christ. We present the Lord and the Spirit does the real winning. We make the introduction and men have to decide whether or not they want Him — but that is their own business. They answer to God for that decision."**

"We are here to learn how to GO. You can't go unless you know. And when you do, you go to fish. But you can't put the fish on the hook. You can put the hook in the water, but the fish have got to bite. (Pause.) Well, if anyone gets the answer, I am willing to change my mind on this, but it looks as if the Holy Spirit is the One who WINS souls and we are called to be faithful."

> HINT: This break-exercise is enjoyable. Your people begin to laugh as you reflect back, "Wise, yes; preach, yes; make disciples, yes, etc." There are more verses, of course, than those mentioned and your audience will delight in the way you handle them. Have a big smile on your face and half-way indicate you have doubts about all this, but just wondering. Of course, the command to win souls is IMPLIED in all these verses. You are using a literal treatment to spotlight the work of the Holy Spirit and present a tension-break at the same time.

WARNINGS FOR THE SOUL-WINNER

● If you can find a road-construction blinker that flashes a yellow light, or a blinking flashlight with an amber lens (or even cellophane over a flashlight will do), hold it toward the audience and blink a few times before asking, **"When you see a flashing amber light, what does it usually mean?"** The answer will come, "It means caution or watch out for something."

"That's correct. And there are five of these lights for the soul-winner. Here's the first one."

> HINT: Prepare flashboards for each of the five warnings and leave the proper one in the chalk-rail while discussing it.

Hold it up first to introduce the caution and then place it in the chalk-rail or the easel during the discussion. Blink your light as an introduction to each of the five warnings.

1. **Get the prospect alone.** If at all possible, people should be dealt with privately. If working in a crusade or inquiry room, deal with a single prospect. However, a man and wife coming together can be treated as a unit. But with teen-agers, it is vital to handle them separately. When another teen-ager is present as an onlooker, your prospect is more concerned with what the other lad is thinking than with what you are saying. Even though you are making a sober presentation of Christ, it usually is turned into a joke. "What will that other fellow think of me if I bow my head and speak to Jesus right here?" is the thought plaguing his mind at the moment; not what he ought to do about his own soul. But deal with him alone and it is a different story.

2. **Stay on target.** This is but another way of saying, ignore interruptions. Satan stirs when a soul-winner begins to work with a prospect and he has many devices calculated to thwart the plan. You can be dealing with a man and suddenly he asks an unrelated question. Usually, these can be dismissed with, "That's a good question, but let's see this first and then I'll answer your question," and go right on with the plan. Questions are often smoke screens. And if you can set them aside for the moment, they will be forgotten when your man has met Christ.

You can be sailing along with your plan and . . . boom. Out of a clear sky comes the question. But more serious, it's often a trap. "What does the Bible say about the Atom bomb?", or, "Is there life on the other planets according to the Bible?", or, "What about Communism, does the Bible say it will win or lose?" —now notice. The questions are usually subjects **about which you know a great deal,** and you must pass up the temptation to display your Bible knowledge and stay on the target!

> HINT: Your audience will appreciate the point when you say, "I blush when I think how often I have bitten on that one. Here comes a question and boy, am I loaded. I spend the time showing off how much I know about the topic and the prospect goes away without Christ. Satan rubs his hands, his plan has worked on me."

THE WARNINGS NEED VISUALS TOO.

3. **Do not defend the Bible.** The Bible is the Sword of the Spirit. It is God's Word, He wrote it, let Him defend it. If it is a "sword," then it is a weapon and weapons are not defended — **they are used.**

> Note: The illustration set forth on page 35 of the soul-winning text is very effective in making this point. If there is a fire extinguisher available, hold it up as you show how ridiculous it would be to explain it when the building was on fire.

4. **Learn to distinguish between resistance and resentment.** These two terms are not the same. There is always some resistance. People are continually resisting the Holy Spirit or they would have been saved long before. Thus, one can expect to meet some resistance when talking to people about Christ. But as you begin to deal with them, should you notice any **hostility** creep into the interview, watch it carefully. There can be resistance, without hostility.

But as soon as the conversation shows signs of becoming hostile, the resistance has changed to resentment.

What happens then? Stop your plan — FAST! Let your eyes take a 3-second inventory of the prospect and locate something worthy of praise and shift the conversation back to him. The plan is halted and the conversation becomes most pleasant. This allows the interview to end with warm, cordial feelings and leaves the door open for a later dealing. If the prospect can remain sweet toward the worker, he will not despise the message. The Holy Spirit's wooing work is done in a **sweet atmosphere,** while His judgmental work is done in a **hostile atmosphere.**

5. **Do not teach a Bible lesson in the middle of an introduction**.
This caution is not found in their soul-winning text. Blink your light and hold up the flash card. Let them tell you what it says.

"In this class we are learning how to INTRODUCE people to Christ. The whole encounter is basically an introduction, isn't it? Therefore, should we stop in the middle of an introduction to teach a Bible lesson? That is no way to introduce anyone. And since we have a long way to go, there are many tempting spots for Bible students to pause and begin a Bible lesson."

● One could stop at every one of the steps of this plan and bring in a host of verses that make lovely teaching. For instance, when the cross is mentioned, what a temptation to recall, "God commendeth His love toward us, that while we were yet sinners, Christ died for us" (Rom. 5:8), as well as many others. But that has to be avoided . That is not our mission at the moment. We are not **convincing** them anything, we are **confronting** them with Someone. That is the objective.

"And people, what about the place where sin is mentioned? My, doesn't the Word have serious things to say at that point? But we must not teach a Bible lesson. When it comes to sin, they are already sensitive to it, did you know that? It is said of the

Holy Spirit, 'When He is come, He will reprove THE WORLD of sin . . . ' (Jo. 16:8). This is His work and accummulated verses on the subject are not necessary when you are working in His power.

> HINT: Demonstrate the sin-sensitivity with the example of going to a doctor. When he probes, he asks, "Does it hurt here? Here? Or here . . . ? "As you touch the last spot, double up in front of your audience and utter a sudden, loud groan. They will laugh, but the matter of sin-sensitivity is established. The world is already "sore" at that point and we need only touch it on our way to present the Remedy. We do not build a case for sin — or anything else in an introduction.

"I think it can be repeated, people, the more we do, the less the Holy Spirit is able to do. So often we find ourselves trying to do His work . . . and can we, class? ("No.") This is what makes soul-winning hard — trying to do the work of the Holy Spirit. So, in this class, we are learning something of GETTING OUT OF HIS WAY and letting Him do the work only He can do."

> ILLUS: Not long ago a man told me, "Boy, we had a real salvation down at the church the other night. I worked two hours with a man and finally brought him through." "Through what?" I thought to myself, "Either that fellow was awfully dense or the worker did not know how to work with the Holy Spirit." It does not take long to make an introduction. If Jesus is honestly and clearly presented at the door of a human heart, He cannot be ignored. The Holy Spirit will not permit it. It is so urgent to learn to work with Him.

ACTION

Have the ushers quickly pass out the 3 x 5 outline cards of the soul-winning plan. When each has received a card, have him hold it before him and prepare to recite the 3 approach questions in unison.

"Now that everyone has a card, we will go through the 3 approach questions together. All right, hold your cards before you and let's do number one. 'Are you interested in spiritual things?' Good. Number two. 'Have you . . . etc.' "

> HINT: Sometimes a prospect responds to the number two question with, "Why, I am a Christian!" But you are suspicious, so you say, "Fine. That's wonderful. I'm interested. Tell me about it, when did you become a Christian?" He may say, "I have been a

Christian all my life." But you are still suspicious, so you ask the number three question, "That's great. And what if someone were to ask you, 'What is a Christian?' what would you say?" Now the X-Ray machine is ticking and you can measure them against the salvation experience.

NOTE: It is possible to escort someone all the way through the salvation encounter and find they have received Christ already. You still have made a good investment. While they have had an experience with Christ in the past, they still are not able to put it into words. So you end up establishing a little one. Now he will know he is saved and why. You have been used greatly.

● Call for your man to come and stand beside you. You are ready to demonstrate the plan once more. This time they are to follow on their cards. They will watch and this time, take mental notes as they observe the flow of the plan and follow the outline on the card. The card becomes an intermediate step as the skill passes from demo, to card, to their hearts.

* * * *

As you bring the demo this time, let them recite the four verses and some of the key phrases. Make brief pauses in your demo for their participation.

* * * *

DRAMA: As you come to the place where Christ is presented, the atmosphere changes. Your audience becomes terribly silent. Your own heart pounds with acceleration. You have just said to your helper, "The Lord Jesus is waiting to come into your heart right now. Will you open the door? Will you let Him in?" Retain the sacredness of the moment as you turn to the class to observe, "**DO YOU FEEL THE PRESENCE OF GOD, RIGHT NOW? DON'T ANSWER, I KNOW YOU DO. EVEN IN A DEMONSTRATION, THE WITNESS OF THE SPIRIT IS NOTICEABLE AT THIS POINT.**" Your people will be thrilled to find the witness of God's presence so real.

LAB WORK

"Now it's your turn to go to work. All have your cards? **Hold them up and wave them** (A precious rustle fills the room and this bit of action is their start.) **All right, now will you turn in your seats to face your neighbor and prepare to go to work for a few minutes. You will each have about 7 minutes for a turn.**

> CAUTION: Instruct them not to be difficult, but do all they can to make it easy for each other. The point is to get through the plan and learn it, not deal with awkward situations. Tell them they can expect to be clumsy and feel stupid, this is natural. Also, they can refer to their book and use the card as much as they like.

"Begin with the phrase, 'God says in His Word that we are all sinners,' and end with 'Bow your head with me.' Take your partner through the short prayer at the end. Now, if you run into problems, lift your hand and I will come over to you. If you can get through it here, you can do it any place. Here it is artificial and somewhat threatening, so just be happy to get through it somehow."

● You may have to jar them a bit to get going. If you are on a platform, you might step down and go to a couple and say, "You work with him." Even put your hand on a man's shoulder as you say this. Then go to another couple and do the same. This starts things off and soon the room sounds like a sawmill. What a glorious buzz! And the timid ones are very grateful for the precious noise that covers their feeble attempts.

> NOTE: Once they start, turn your back on them and get busy with the supplies on your table. With your stare removed, they become bold. In minutes they forget all about you until they need to ask a question. Then you can be looking for raised hands. When the time is gone, you have to break it up, but get pictures first. They're great.

"All right, our time is gone. (They begin to settle and the din subsides.) **Now the next time you see the plan demonstrated, you will know what things to look for, won't you? And by now you have discovered what a help those transition lines really are."** (Usually a question or two is raised here.)

ASSIGNMENT

"Now here's your assignment. Will you invite a neighbor in for a cup of coffee sometime this week and explain that you are attending a class at church and the teacher told you to invite

A LITTLE NEW AT THE START . . .

. . . BUT THEN IT GETS EASIER.

him in and practice on him. Lay the full blame or responsibility on me. Say I told you to do it. And then get ready for a surprise. When it comes time to say, "Jesus is at the door of your heart; will you let Him in?" switch your role a bit and say, "This is more than just practice, Jesus really is at your heart-door right now, wouldn't you like to invite Him in?" All of a sudden you will find the Holy Spirit does all these wonderful things I have been telling you. And some of you will have stories for us next time, I know."

"Also, I want you to finish reading the soul-winning book. There are some very important things there I will not be teaching in this class. Particularly should you become familiar with the discussion on repentance. It's an eye-opener."

Prayer—Dismiss

WHAT TO BRING

1. Flash cards
2. Supply of 3 x 5 cards
3. Extra books and folder for newcomers
4. Camera
5. Optional—(fire extinguisher)
6. Chalk and eraser
7. Blackboard
8. Yellow flashing light

Chapter Four
BACK TO THE LAB
THIS SESSION YOU:
- Re-emphasize the Spirit's work by review.
- Discuss God's estimate of personal soul-winning.
- Demonstrate—the class follows in unison.

GREETING
You may wish to lead in prayer again, for later you will be speaking of Satan and want the Lord to keep you from the Evil One during the hour. He will seek to upset your ministry, for he dreads any session where he receives attention. Loving darkness, he will try to put out a spotlight focused on him. The people are settled and ready for your story.

STORY
In one of the Eastern deserts is a guide who never loses his way. There is a special pocket inside his loose shirt where he carries a homing pigeon with a very fine cord attached to one leg. To check his way, he merely releases the bird who strains at the cord in the direction of home. They call him the "Dove Man."

Apply:

"The effective soul-winner must become a Dove man. As the desert guide trusts the pigeon for direction, so does the soul-winner fully trust the Dove of God (Holy Spirit) for His ministry. Last time, it may have occurred to some we went overboard on the ministry of the Holy Spirit. But can this really be so, when all we are learning is no good apart from Him?"

REVIEW
"So this is not really a seminar in which we are only learning a method. In fact, we are learning more than a plan, aren't we? And as I ask these things, feel free to respond. Get ready for your "A's" and remember anyone can sound off."

1. "We are learning a plan for . . . what?" (Ans. Working with the Holy Spirit.)

RECALL: In this class you are teaching more than a method — the skill of moving in the power of God. They are learning to work with the Spirit in bringing men face to face with Jesus. The great apostasy, predicted for the end time, is here, only it is wearing a religious mask. And for men to be saved, it takes a face-to-face encounter with Jesus, or they will hide behind the religious smoke screen and remain in their lost condition.

2. **"Last time we showed how we travel in steps to bring men face-to-face with Jesus.** (Step to the board and indicate.) **And while we said our work was SYSTEMATIC, we described the work of the Spirit as . . . what?"** (Ans. **Automatic.**) **"Name several things the Holy Spirit does automatically?"**

RECALL: He convicts of sin: bear witness to the winner's intentions; authenticates the Word of God; verifies the wages of sin; makes Christ real upon presentation and pierces the prospect's heart with the challenge.

NOTE: With chalk in hand, check off on the board each step as the class calls the Spirit's work. This provides your students with a mental image of the Spirit's operation.

RECALL: We move systematically because we have a long way to go. When we contact a man we do not know what is on his mind. We have to approach him and create a spiritual climate. Then we escort him all the way to the place where he can consider Christ at the door of his heart, intellectually. While we travel this distance, the Holy Spirit bears witness each step of the way . . . AUTOMATICALLY.

3. **"Then we had 5 flashing yellow lights; cautions. Name them."** (Ans. Get the subject alone; stay on target; don't defend the Bible; learn to distinguish between resistance and resentment and do not teach a Bible lesson in the middle of an intro.)

STORY: Once, after a seminar where the caution against teaching a Bible Lesson was forcibly brought out, a man hurried forward to speak to me. He gripped my hand and with tears on his cheeks said, "Brother Lovett, I have been a Bible teacher for 30 years. I want you to know Satan has used this very thing to keep me from introducing men to Jesus. Let me confess, I have often worked in crusades and now I see the awful thing that has happened. After the evangelist had done his work and the people came forward, I took them into the inquiry room and preached another sermon. I didn't realize until now, the devil used my Bible knowledge to make me ineffective. I can see why so many I dealt with never remained in the faith. I am grateful for what I have learned here and guarantee that tragedy won't happen again, now."

NEW MATERIAL

"We began this session asking God to protect us from the 'wicked one,' because Satan hates what we're doing now. He is furious over the ministry and resents the fact you are acquiring God's best method for bringing men to Himself. Now by best method, I do not mean the plan itself, but the PERSONAL METHOD."

● The personal method is God's best. One might ask, "Doesn't Satan hate the radio, T.V. and preachers, particularly those like Billy Graham?" Yes, but the man in the crowd can easily ignore the public challenge and besides, there are multitudes who will never be a part of any evangelistic crowd. Many will never turn on a Gospel program or come near a meeting. How will they be reached? God has a way — **Personal messengers.**

> STORY: When I was with the Air Force in India, our squadron was called to attention one day and the officer in charge said, "Gentlemen, may I present the Commander of the China-Burma-India Theatre." As I stood there with the others, I couldn't honestly feel I had met the man. But minutes later, a fellow officer took me by the arm and presented me personally, "Captain Lovett, I'd like you to meet General ...." I shook his hand and shortly after became his personal pilot. I met him and then served him. And so it is with Christ. In the crowd it is more like hearing ABOUT Him, than meeting Him. But face-to-face, it is a personal encounter.

● When you think about it, the personal method is the most polite way to invite men. What could be more polite than a servant who conveys the good wishes of his master? Could it be more clear? And surely, in a private moment, it is the least embarrassing. And what about questions? Why, the personal messenger can even take care of those. No, it is by far the best way.

"Therefore Satan hates a seminar where people are trained to go get 'em. And he hates you. You know your name is written in the 'Lamb's Book of Life,' but it is also written in Satan's book, too. Oh yes, he keeps books. And there's a special mark by your name now. You are to get special attention because of this experience and he is going to see that you have a filling of his spirit. Shocked? Did you not know there is a filling of the unholy spirit!"

● The filling of the unholy spirit produces its own fruit in the life. A man filled with this spirit is a man of fear. Satan can fill you with fear. Also, he can fill your life with things to do and lead you to believe they are more important than, "Follow Me." He can fill you with procrastination and excuses to go with it. He can fill you with doubts as to your calling and flood your soul with ideas of personal inadequacy for soul-winning. He can fill your life with critical friends who challenge any form of aggressiveness for Jesus.

"But people, all fishermen are aggressive. They get up at 4 a.m., will sleep all night in a car, spend all day in a sun-baked boat, squander good sums for tackle, go hungry, get dirty, slide down steep banks and scale them again, even waste whole days — just to catch fish. No, don't let anyone tell you aggressiveness isn't normal for fishermen."

ACTION

"Will you take your copies of the soul-winning book and once more turn to page 110 where we found the 7 transition lines. Got them? All right, let's recite them again . . . 'If it is OK with you . . . '"

● Go down the list with them. As you stagger the phrasing it sounds much like responsive reading in some worship services. The exercise, while childishly simple, cements the lines and attaches an unusual emotion to them. A class, reciting like this, unconsciously makes the material common property. The students feel they have the words in common and are not ashamed to work with them in the lab session. They know by now the recitals are valuable.

DEMO

"Now I will ask Mr._____to stand here with me and we will go through the plan again. I know you will be watching closely, for in a few minutes, you will be turning in your seats to work with your neighbor. You have already made one clumsy attempt, haven't you? (Humorously) And so you will be looking for those gaps or things you missed in your last practice. Those memory traces will be etched a bit deeper as we see it again."

● You are standing there with your helper and just before you begin, you ask the students, **"We will start the demonstration with your asking the approach questions. Let's say them together.** (Lift your hand as a baton and lead them.) **'Are you interested in Spiritual things?'** . . . **Good. Number Two, 'Have** . . . (they will supply the rest.) . . . **Fine. Number 3, 'If someone . . . ' Thank you. Now we will begin in the same place as you will, with the words . . .**

'God says in His Word that we are all sinners . . .'"

* * * *

Again, this space is reserved for the demonstration. Pause in the plan at key points and ask the group to repeat strategic lines after you. Check the recording to see how this is done.

* * * *

LAB WORK

"Now it is time for you to work. There will be at least 20 minutes, and if things go well, each will have a turn. Do you feel a little afraid? (Nod your head. It is good psychology for them to admit fears.) **Satan is doing his best to frighten you, for he dreads the thought of your becoming soul-winners. You will feel** foolish, a bit awkward, nervous and inadequate as you turn to your partner. Maybe your mind will go blank. (Wait for nervous laughter to escape.) **Expect this. But also notice this: THE MOMENT YOU TRY, it all changes. Do you recall the verse, "Resist the devil and he will flee from you?" Good, I'm glad you do. For you are about to prove this verse in actual experience. The moment you begin, the fears will depart and you will enjoy yourselves. See if this isn't so."**

"Do you all have a card outline? Hold them up. Wave them. (Again that precious rustle fills the room and your people have begun to move. Clap your hands and the popping sound will serve as a signal.) **It is time to go to work."**

● Once they are under way, you can turn to observe their work. Now they are busy and will not notice your gaze. Some will show good progress, having read and reread their books. Others have practiced the plan in their eagerness to learn. But some will have difficulty and hands will go up. Walk over to them to give what help is needed. Don't forget the pictures. Get some of those intimate scenes.

"All right people, we have about 2 minutes more. (That jars them a bit and they pause to look up. But you turn away again and spend those minutes getting ready for the assignment.) **Time's up . . .** (they settle now) **. . . and I want to give the assignment. But first, notice what happened in this lab work. You were a bit wary to begin, weren't you? But after you started, it was fun to work together. Well, the same holds true in soul-winning. It seems frightening at first, but after you have started, it becomes enjoyable. Satan's hold is broken, once you start to obey. Someone has likened this to stepping into a lion's den, only to discover the lion has RUBBER TEETH."**

YOUNG PEOPLE CATCH ON FAST . . .

. . . OLDER ONES LEARN TO WIN TOO.

ASSIGNMENT

"How are you coming with your coffee-cup evangelism? Any results to report? (A hand or two may go up.) **We will continue with this same assignment and those who did not get an opportunity last week, will want to give it a try. It doesn't have to be at home. You men can try the same thing at lunch. Get one of the fellows with whom you work, to go to lunch with you. Afterwards, lay the blame on me as you tell him of your practice assignment. He'll go along with you."**

> EXPERIENCE: In nearly every seminar where I have given this assignment, someone has reported a thrilling story. Generally, it runs like this: "I did just as you said, but when I tried the plan I was so clumsy. I forgot part and had to look in the book and I would have been lost without the card. But somehow I got through it and do you know what? My friend told me he had been wanting to do this for a long time, but didn't know how! He invited Jesus to come into his heart and I believe he was honestly saved!"

"Next time we will be discussing **F-E-A-R** in soul-winning. There is such a thing, you know. (Laughter at this.) **You may want to take notes. And now may we ask the Holy Spirit to seal the things we have done in His presence tonight."**

> NOTE: With this lesson and those to follow, minimum time is spent on lecture and the lab receives the greater emphasis. It is in the lab the students really learn. The more familiar they can become with the plan, the more certain is your investment in them.

Prayer—Dismiss.

WHAT TO BRING

1. Supply of 3 x 5 cards for those who forget.
2. Extra books for newcomers
3. Flash cards (optional)
4. Camera
5. Blinking light (optional)

Chapter Five

FEAR - - - IT'S GOT TO GO!

THIS TIME YOU WANT TO:
- Review the highlights of the Encounter-Method
- Discuss the matter of fear
- Spend as much time as possible in the lab

GREETING

Prayer brings the room to quiet. You sense the stories waiting to come out as a result of your last assignment. This should be an exciting session, but you have a story too. They would be disappointed if you didn't.

"Last time we promised to discuss the subject of fear. But who can tell me, what is the opposite of fear? (Ans. Peace.) **That's right. And may we begin with an incident that sets forth the real nature of peace."**

STORY

A contest was held in England where artists were asked to compete for a prize in depicting "Peace." In time, the judging began. Two pictures ended as finalists, but only one could win. The first was a beautiful landscape of the English countryside with all at rest. No wind stirred the golden harvest in the fields. The green hills provided background for brightly colored huts and even the cattle appeared contented. But it did not get the prize. No, the winning picture was filled with action. It was a storm scene. Lightning flashed against black skies as rain fell upon a huge tree. Chilling winds beat back the branches to expose a mother bird upon her nest. And there, huddled beneath the protecting wings of their mother, were her babies. The little eyes showed no fear and they snuggled under her warm wings and peered out. That was peace—peace in the midst of storm. That is real peace.

Apply:

"And that is the peace of the soul-winner. True peace as the Holy Spirit demonstrates His faithfulness, in the midst of Satan's fury, to take our surrender and use it for the salvation of souls. It helps to know this, but one can only know it after he has proved the Lord. Therefore, I want to give you some things that will help even before you get started. We'll have those in a moment, but first let's see what is soaking in."

REVIEW QUESTIONS

"This time make it a real popcorn review. As soon as I speak, someone pop up with the answer. We'll go back over the whole encounter method. All set? Fine."

1. **"Salvation is in a . . . ?"** (Ans. Person.)
2. **"Soul-winning is . . . what?"** (Ans. An introduction, Introducing that Person.)
3. **"To be effective we need . . . what?"** (Ans. A Plan.)
4. **"Why do we need a plan or method?"** (Ans. Distance we travel requires it.)
5. **"We are learning more than a method. It is also the skill of . . . what?"** (Ans. Working with the Holy Spirit.)
6. **"Any soul-winning technique must consider two things . . . name one?"** (Ans. The Person of Christ . . . and . . . The Nature of Man.)
7. **"We have said, that while our work was . . . what? The work of the Holy Spirit is . . . what?"** (Ans. Systematic - Automatic.)
8. **"Can you name the five cautions?"** (Ans. Get subject alone, stay on target, don't defend the Bible, distinguish between resistance and resentment, and do not teach a Bible lesson in the middle of an introduction.)
9. **"Who can tell me the things the Holy Spirit does automatically when we begin to deal with someone?"** (Ans. Bears witness to your intentions, authenticates the Word of God, verifies the wages of sin, makes Christ real, and seals the challenge to the prospect's heart.)

10. "**And what was the assignment last time?**" (Ans. Coffee-cup evangelism.)

"**Oh, you are doing fine. I am getting prouder of you each session. I see the material is soaking in. Now what about the coffee-cup assignment?** (Look for indications among the people.) **Anything to report?**"

> NOTE: If there are stories, let them come out. If there are none, counter with, "MAYBE SOME OF YOU HAVE QUESTIONS YOU WISH TO ASK OF ME, INSTEAD." (Often, they do have questions.) "IT CAN BE YOUR TURN NOW."

● There are two questions asked continually:

1. "Whenever I tell someone Christ is waiting to come into his heart, the reply is, 'What do you mean, my heart? It's just a muscle that pumps blood.' How do I answer them?"

> ANSWER: Say to them, "I mean, what you mean, when you tell your wife or girlfriend, you love her with all your heart."
> The reply to that will be, "Oh."

2. "I used the approach questions with a man and the first thing he said to me was, 'I'm a Catholic.' I didn't know what to say next."

> ANSWER: Say to him, "Are you a born-again Catholic?" He will ask, "What do you mean?" Then whip open your Testament to John 1:12, "Here's what I mean . . . (read the verse) . . . God says we need to receive Christ in order to be His sons. And when we become the sons of God we are born again." He may reply, "I do receive Christ. I receive Him every time I take Communion." Then answer soberly, "Oh, I don't mean into your STOMACH, I mean into your HEART." He will stagger for an instant and in that opportunity press, "He's waiting to come into your heart right now . . . listen to this . . . (flip to Rev. 3:20 and read and press for the decision) . . . will you let Him in?" This is every effective.

NEW MATERIAL

The questions are finished and you are happy with the progress of the class. You have covered a lot of ground and the important insights of the soul-winning encounter have become their property. From now on, you will be reinforcing the material and helping them to put it into operation. Even the material you are now to present is not new, but arranged to bridge the gap between the classroom and the "firing line."

NOTE: Spend minimum time with this new material. Too much time here will rob them of the best part — the lab work. Take a look at the clock and determine how much of the following can be presented and select that which will help most.

"**Now I am going to say a bad word.** (Let your hands tremble as you overact the shaking of someone afraid.) **. . . and that bad word is F-E-A-R. W-w-hat does that spell? Right, and it is real, isn't it?** (You won't have to nod your head this time.) **There are some insights that can help us when it comes to fear."**

● Your students may not realize it, but their own lab practice is the greatest single aid. As you have already pointed out, people fear things they do not know. And when they have mastered the plan where there is no more struggle for words, much fear is automatically removed. Part of the fear comes from worry over what to say.

● **Use the passive approach.** (Check page 124 of the soul-winning book.) Newly trained workers are frequently haunted by the idea; "Now that I am trained and have the skill, am I expected to button-hole everyone I meet and lead him to Christ?" If you suggest the passive approach for their beginning, a sigh of relief will pass through the class. Both the passive and the aggressive are Scriptural. But they will relax with the suggestion of starting out in the soul-winning business much as a new doctor begins his practice and waits for people to come to him.

NOTE: But you are not suggesting they stay home and say, "Lord send some soul to me today," and do nothing about it themselves. No, they will have to be like the new doctor opening his office. They will need to hang out a "shingle" and advertise or people will not know of their ministry. Suggest things as, cultivating their speech with, "Lord willing, I will do thus and so," or having a New Testament on the desk at work, or handing out a few tracts to mark them as people of God. Then the prospects will come when they have need.

- **Expect Refusals.** Rejectors are refusing Christ, not you. The program of God is based on man's freewill response and "whosoever will may come." While God would that none should perish, most mankind is traveling the broad way to destruction, "for strait is the gate and narrow is the way that leadeth unto life, and **FEW** there be that find it."

Therefore, do not let refusals upset you. You are merely an introducer. You present Christ and people do what they will with Him, but they are judged for it. No one is a successful soul-winner because he wins souls. A successful worker is one who presents the Lord **faithfully** and allows people to do what they will with Him. There is no such thing as a good soul-winner. All that is required is a clear presentation and the real work is done by the Holy Spirit.

- **Start as an inquiry room worker.** Soul-winning is not the same thing as working at the altar or the inquiry room. There, a professional minister has done the hard part in securing the person's response and respondents come forward ready to do business with Christ. All that is needed is someone who can introduce them to Jesus with clearness. In soul-winning, however, one must "do the work of an evangelist." This means, he has to create the religious climate, bring the matter of sin to the prospect's heart, offer the gift of life in Christ, explain the receipt of Jesus and press for a decision. But in the inquiry room or altar, this has all been done for the worker. Thus it is a wonderful place to gain experience in closing the deal with people who are eager. It is a place of **reduced threat** and offers beginners bite-sized experience.

- **Get into visitation.** Visitation takes one **systematically** into people's homes every week. And you are there on spiritual business. If you have some fears and want to creep up on this business of being a soul-winner, volunteer to serve as the silent partner in visitation. Here you will gain first hand experience within the soul-winning situation without actually handling the prospect. You will see the Holy Spirit work before your eyes and witness His ministry upon the prospect's heart. Then, after a time, it will be an easy step to the role of the prime visitor. Doing it this way allows you to digest a bulk of the fear even before you begin to deal with anyone. From there on, you can do it without intense fear.

> **EXPERIENCE:** I recall being in a home expecting the visit to be a brief one. I was glad, because I wanted to get home and see a certain television show. But the man was interested in spiritual things and hungry to have me stay. "Oh, oh, I thought to myself. This is going to keep me here awhile." He mentioned problems, but it was soon obvious he was insisting I introduce him to Jesus. Visitation can be like that. There are times when you would have to work to keep from winning souls.

● Soul-winning is not unlike getting into a swimming pool. Some people know it's going to be cold, and bracing themselves for the shock, plunge right in. After awhile, the water seems warm. Others, not so bold, cautiously climb down the ladder one step at a time. That's all right too. They can go from the inquiry room — to the silent partner in visitation — to becoming a soul-winning visitor in successive steps. No two are alike, so it is best for people to perform according to their personality strengths.

● Do not hesitate to mention visitation. This is a most precious work of the local church, since it permits everyone "to get into the act." Done at the three levels, i.e., Caller-centered (social), Church-centered and Christ-centered, visitation is the place for even the most timid to get active for Christ. And what wonderful discipline for the trained soul-winner! Week after week, he finds himself faced with opportunities and is forced to be productive.

NOTE: Teaching people to win souls and then leaving them to their own resources, is to invite poor results. They may or may not deal with people by this promiscuous means. But make them a part of systematic visitation and they will reach people the year 'round. Thus it can be said, visitation is the proper discipline for the trained soul-winner.

HINT: If your class contains pastors, hold up a copy of "Visitation Made Easy," and give a taste of the know-how it offers. Pull a photo album from your pocket and say to them, "This album and the visitation plan of this book can bring 5 new families into your church every week." This is a good investment if you can get some pastors to take a serious peek at visitation. All the great churches of our country have made their gains through visitation. And this is because God loves to use His people in reaching out to a community.

"These things taken seriously, can rid you of 90% of your soul-winning fear. It is not good to remove it all. For true excitement always has a dash of fear for spice. Even a roller-coaster ride has a fragment of fear, or it could never be so thrilling. And the same is true of hunting, skiing or anything else. So we want to leave enough fear for soul-winning to be the adventure it promises to be."

LAB WORK

● People want to ask questions now. Not because they seek answers, but all this talk of fear has aroused feelings and they would like to stall off having to work. Even without your asking, hands will probably go up now and one or two will start the ball rolling for a round of questions. But you are wise to them and can tell them so.

"**All right youse guys, I know yez is askin questions to keep from goin to woik. But I am wise to yuh, see.**" (Give this an Edward G. Robinson flavor and their laughter will explode. When it settles you continue:) **I know you are ready, so please remember this is a class for making things easy. In our lab work we do not want to make it difficult for the partner. We want him to get through it as easily as possible in order to learn it. So if you have to help one another a bit, do it. This isn't cheating, unless we're cheating Satan.**"

NOTE: There may be "first timers" show up even though this is the fifth session. Word spreads fast when it is rumored practical know-how is available. And people will come great distances hoping to glean even a fragment of help, fully aware they have missed most of the material. Team these with people who show the best promise. Not only does it give them a nice exposure to the skill, but some will be very earnest and eat up every word in their zeal.

- **If you have time,** give them another demonstration. Now skip all the side comments and go straight through the plan. If you have access to a cassette player, use the demonstration cassette, if you like, to save your voice. After the cassette has been played, don't let them get started with questions, unless it is obvious something vital has been overlooked.

"This time we are going to have 25 minutes, which means each partner should get through the plan without any strain. I'll be somewhere around the front of the room and if you run into trouble, just raise your hand and I will come over to you. Okay, let's go to work . . ."

BY NOW THE LAB IS FUN — AND EASY!

HINT: Turn your back upon the audience with those words and they will accept it as a signal to get busy. If they just sit, which is unlikely by now, go through the same procedure you used before. Personally instruct a pair to work together and without waiting for their reaction, go to another couple, etc. They will get under way. This time you can look around the room and rejoice in the fruit of of your investment. Real soul-winners are showing up as the result of your labors.

ASSIGNMENT

● Order has been restored and you address them again.

"You're doing fine. Maybe more of you will be coffee-cup evangelists this week. You see I am not going to let up. Be sure to tell them it is my fault you are practising on them."

NOTE: If some have come from other churches, and are there for the first time, take a minute to hold up the pink folder for their sake. Tell them, "SOME OF YOU ARE FROM OTHER CHURCHES AND WE WOULD LIKE TO SHARE WITH YOUR PASTORS WHAT WE ARE DOING HERE. IF YOU WOULD CARE TO SEE ME AFTER CLASS, I WANT TO GIVE ONE OF THESE PANORAMAS TO TAKE ALONG AND SHOW TO HIM." When they speak to you about the folder, perhaps you can persuade them to secure a soul-winning book to show to him too. This is a way of getting word of your ministry out to other churches.

"Next time will be our last session. Won't you practice this week, so that any flaws in your technique will show up and we can care for them. There will be one more demonstration and it will allow you to pick up the fine points missing in your presentation right now."

Prayer—Dismiss

NOTE: After class stand at your table. If you played the cassette during this session, some will ask to buy one from you. Encourage them to do this for it is a precious aid in memorizing the plan. A housewife, for example, can play it over and over while she is ironing and fix the dialogue in her heart. For some, this will be the only way they can master it.

WHAT TO BRING

1. Cassette player and cassettes
2. Blackboard
3. Breath sweetner for interviews
4. Camera

Chapter Six

GET 'EM GOING

FINALLY, YOU WANT TO:
- Polish the rough edges
- Acknowledge faithful attendance (certificates)
- Challenge the students to action

GREETING

"After tonight, you will behold my face no more. Recall how the elders of Miletus felt when Paul said goodbye to them. They sorrowed, because he said they should see his face no more. I trust it will not be that way with us, but should you not see me again, you will hear my voice in your imagination as you read the book. It should remind you of the times we have had here together."

STORY

When our Lord Jesus was crucified, two prominent Jews did a surprising thing. These were outstanding members of the Sanhedrin and no one would have guessed they would be the ones to step forward and save the body of Jesus from a criminal burial. One was the rich Joseph of Arimathea, a timid man, who had prepared the tomb for himself and the other was Nicodemus, who came to Jesus at night for a private interview.

At a moment when none of Jesus' disciples dared move, these defied the council of Jerusalem and risked their reputations to take the body of Jesus. And if they touched that corpse, what a daring thing for Jews right before the Passover! Think of it! When the rest of the world was sneering at Christ, these were willing to become outcasts with Him. Fools? Surely they looked it, for it must have cost all they had. But then came the Resurrection. How do you think they felt then? And what must have been their joy that morning!

Apply:

But what of today? Is it any different now? Is Jesus any more popular? No, even though Christianity has been around 2000 years, the world is still unimpressed with Jesus. While religion is popular, He isn't. Mention His name in public and what happens? Even the "religious" people are shocked. So it is still a time of humiliation for our Lord.

Oh, but what an opportunity for us. We know a day of Glory is coming. And if we hold back now in the day of His unpopularity, how will we feel in the day of His revelation! That is why this class means so much. You are learning to speak out for Jesus in a day when His Name on your lips can be a shock. When He returns with all the Holy Angels, He will be the center of every conversation. Your witness will be too late then.

"This class equips you to dare to be Nicodemuses and Josephs. Now you can minister in the face of His modern reproach and startle men with His Name. I know you will agree with me (and with Nic and Joe) **that it is better to be ashamed before men now, than before HIM — THEN!"**

REVIEW

None. Time used for the challenge.

FINAL DEMONSTRATION

● Motion for your man to come and stand beside you. You will begin an uninterrupted demo. This time eyes and ears strain to catch any fine points missed in practice sessions.

"This time as you watch the demonstration you will be sensitive to certain points that troubled you in practice. On your 3 x 5 cards there is room to write in key words or thoughts that will aid in smoothness. Look at your card as we travel the steps and try to recall the parts that were difficult for you."

* * * *

Space reserved for demo. Let them recite the 3 approach questions as a kick-off.

ACTION

"All right, it's your turn now. I know I don't have to caution you on making it easy for each other. So now, prepare to work with your partner. If some of you want to work with someone in particular, that is OK too. All have your cards? Let's see them. **Wave them.** (again the atmosphere is charmed with that ice-breaking sound.) **Fine. Begin with the line, 'God says in His Word that we are all sinners.' Got it? Let's go."**

● Let them work as long as possible. Call out when the time is half gone as a signal to change partners. Announce it as time to give the other fellow a turn. Watch that you do not spend too much time with any one team. Others will need your help, but hesitate to raise their hands while you are conversing. Don't let anyone keep you too long with a story. Answer as quickly as possible and keep yourself available.

> **NOTE:** By now you have discovered the two most valuable things in your seminar have been your demonstrations and the time in the lab. Were you severely restricted to time, say only 40 minutes, you would want to have these. They may forget the teaching, but once a skill is acquired you have made a deposit. Your success or failure as a teacher depends on what they gain for Jesus, not how well they were impressed with your ministry.

FINAL WORDS TO YOUR CLASS

"**Our time is gone. We can wind it up now . . .** "
● The buzz subsides as the teams break up and redirect their attention to the front of the room once more. You have a good estimate now of your investment. You take a hasty measurement of the students. Some practiced at home and gained wonderful facility. Maybe they can do it better than you. If so, feel free to glow inside.

" **. . . Well, we have had a good time together and I am pleased with you all. You have been faithful in coming and we want to acknowledge that faithfulness with a certificate.** (Hold up the completion certificate.) **As soon as we are ready to be** dismissed, I would like you to come in single file and let me say goodbye to each of you and present you with your diploma."

> HINT: People love diplomas. This will be the most public stunt required of them, passing in line before you. Since this class prepares people for a private ministry, they are not required to give public demonstrations of the skill. In fact, to have them do so, is contrary to the personal ministry. Many, who can do a fine job in private, freeze at the thought of giving a public demonstration of their ability.

● But now they are to hear your final words. Oh, if only you could leave them with a smoldering challenge to be fanned to fury everytime the pastor or evangelist brought up the matter of winning others to Jesus.

"In the time we have remaining, may I ask if any of you remember a disaster that occurred in this country right after the turn of the Century? It was the great fire of the Iroquois Theatre in 1903. Does anyone remember that fire Or know about it?" (A few heads will nod . . . probably grey ones. They will remember it well.)

STORY

It was a terrible fire which occurred before theatres were required to have fire extinguishers, proper exits and fire proof draperies. The Iroquois was starring Eddie Foy in a big extravaganza and was overcrowded. The fire broke out and seemed to explode in its race to envelop the building. Panic struck almost immediately and people jammed the aisles in a desperate struggle to get to the doors. The hot gasses filling the place made it a death chamber. Over 590 died. It was an awful sight. The strong shoved aside the weak and men literally climbed over the bodies of others as they clawed their way to freedom. Some made their escape over the mountain of bodies barring the exits.

We're interested in the story of one man who got out. He didn't live long afterwards, the horror and shock affected him so.

As he reached the end of his days, he would go into his room and shut the door. His worried family would come and listen only to hear him cry again and again in his agony . . . "I saved no one but myself . . . I saved no one but myself . . . " And he kept it up until he died. What a way to go out of this life!

Apply:

The application is easy. We're in a world that is heading for hell and there are multitudes who do not know Jesus as Saviour and hence cannot escape the destruction ahead. What a terrible thing for men to find Christ and the relief His splendid Salvation brings, but then be faced with . . . "I saved no one but myself." That would be bad wouldn't it? But what sickening feelings must linger inside that person who has been trained to do this very thing — and then makes no attempt to salvage a soul! May God grant that none of you, armed with this know-how, should face his last days in the awful agony of "I saved no one but myself."

"But I have confidence in you. I have seen you work and know the Holy Spirit is waiting to take you on the great adventure of seeing men and women come to Jesus through your ministry. I promise you the time of your lives. What glory explodes in our souls when we personally welcome a brother into the family of God. It is fantastic. This is the legacy I leave you. The promise of our Lord to anoint you with power for soul-winning . . . and now may we commit ourselves to God."

PRAYER. Commit the course and the people to the Holy Spirit.

"And now will you come to receive your diplomas. You are free to go when we have said goodbye."

> NOTE: Some teachers, when the group is small, elect to have a dinner. The diplomas can thus be awarded in special ceremony.

WHAT TO BRING

1. Extra books
2. Diplomas
3. Supplies for soul–winners
4. Camera (award pictures)

"JUST FOR YOU"

There now? Can't you just picture yourself presenting this skill! Maybe you have taught a soul-winning class before. No? Then everything you need is right here in these pages. Ask the Lord to open the door and HE will. Take this very plan of teaching to a group of Christians and you are guaranteed the time of your life. God is eager to bless this work — and that makes it fun. So little is truly known of this science, you will be amazed the way people soak up what you teach.

Won't you weigh the idea before the Lord and see what He indicates? I am sure you will sense His eagerness to help you start. Once you do, you will enjoy a precious anointing. I promise from experience, your talent will be multiplied a hundred times.

QUESTIONS MOST FREQUENTLY ASKED IN CLASSES

Q— "Do you really believe everyone can be a soul-winner?"

A— No, at least not at first. But anyone can be trained for the moment when God sends along the opportunity when anyone could win souls if he knew how. For example, should a bomb drop nearby and you survive, there could be people about you crying to God in agony. Pride wouldn't matter then and neither would clumsiness. At such a time, anyone could win souls . . . **if he knew how.** Thus, every Christian is under obligation to prepare himself. The moment may be closer than we suspect.

Q— "How do you work with someone who has been taken through the plan before, but did not make a decision for Christ?"

A— Here the key phrase is, "and do you remember?" Should you begin to deal with a man where a visitor has called previously and used the plan, simply say, "You remember when he opened his Testament to this verse?" and "Do you recall what he said about our being sinners?" etc., all the way down to, "And he told you Jesus was standing at your heart's door? Well, that's still true. He's waiting to come into your heart, right now. Will you let Him in?"

Q— "Are you not teaching us the same high pressure methods used by salesmen to close a deal? And do we need high pressure tactics?"

A— The tender presentation of Christ at the door of a human heart is the most gentle and delicate means of God in bringing men to Jesus. In fact, it is only polite, as we discussed in one session. A message sent by a personal messenger, who knows how to help people make a decision, is the best means. Now when it comes to high pressure, the Holy Spirit is Master of the Art. People have come forward in meetings crying and broken and declaring it was as though a hand reached out and dragged them. They are broken and under awful conviction. Polio, auto accidents, loss of jobs, martial distress, wayward children, fire tragedies are but a few of the means God allows to serve Him. No, the personal messenger who presents Christ in love, is God's most gentle way. To allow people to go untouched, would be cruel.

Q— "You use the tapping on the heart to bring a reality experience, but what should men do in dealing with women."

A— A man ought not to touch a woman, this is clear. Therefore, if he will take just the tip of his finger and ever so lightly, touch her wrist, it will provide an equivalent "smash" to her heart. The Holy Spirit will allow this and there is never a hint of anything out of order when it is done in Jesus' Name.

Q— "Since you only teach 4 verses in the plan, what place do you give to Scripture memorization?"

A— Since the soul-winning plan is an introduction with the Holy Spirit doing most of the work, these are all that are needed for the truth's sake. But it is not possible to have victory in one's personal life without constant meditation in the Word of God. Scripture memorization is the greatest single step toward that victory. If the Word can flow from one's heart to his mind, it is easier to practice the presence of Jesus. And it is the awareness of Christ's indwelling presence that makes the most dramatic change in our lives.

Q— "Why do you insist on emphasizing the word "receive," when the Bible says, 'Believe on the Lord Jesus Christ and thou shalt be saved?' "

A— I love that verse too. But the word **believe** doesn't mean today what it meant in New Testament times. Today it can be used even to express doubt. A wife, for example, when she is not sure when her husband will arrive, may say, "I believe he will be home around noon."

> HINT: If the point is labored, place a chair before the class and sit on it holding your legs off the floor. Say to the class, "I believe this chair will hold me up, why?" Don't wait for an answer. "Because it is already holding me up and all of my weight is upon it. This is what is meant by the New Testament word, "believe." We believe in Christ because He is saving us as we put all of our weight upon Him and rest in His finished work at Calvary. This is not communicated in the modern use of the word.